RELEVANT SELLING

RELEVANT SELLING

RESEARCH PROVES CUSTOMERS
VALUE MORE THAN JUST PRICE

JAYNIE L. SMITH

International Speaker and Consultant on
Competitive Advantage

with

CRAIG MOWREY and MARK STEISEL

Executive Suite Press, Inc.
New York
Fort Lauderdale

PUBLISHED BY EXECUTIVE SUITE PRESS, INC.

Copyright © 2012 by Jaynie L. Smith
All Rights Reserved

For information about special discounts for bulk purchases, or
speakers on this subject for your event, please contact Smart
Advantage at 954 763 5757

Published in the United States by Executive
Suite Press, Inc,

All trademarks are the property of the
respective companies
Book design by Jonathan Gullery
Jacket design by Ashley Dufrene
Cataloging-in-Publication Data is on file with
the Library of Congress

ISBN – 978-0-615-56403-6

PRINTED IN THE UNITED STATES OF AMERICA

CONTENTS

Acknowledgements

A s is almost always the case in a book as dependent on years of research and analysis as this one, there are many people whom I would like to recognize for their contributions and for making this book possible.

First a special thanks to the countless companies and executives named in our case studies. They persevered through our process and graciously allowed us to share their experiences and outcomes with you.

Many of these companies are members of an elite organization known today as Vistage. It was formerly known as The Executive Committee (TEC). For over twenty years I have had the privilege of being associated with Vistage, a leading international organization of CEOs. Through my speaking engagements, I have been exposed to thousands of incredibly bright and successful

CEOs at their Vistage meetings. Some of my research began with these CEOs, and some of those members are profiled in these stories.

I also have had the privilege of speaking to many national and international associations as a keynote speaker. These interactions provided a treasure trove of reflections, which helped to shape my thought processes and ultimately led to the research that gave birth to this book.

My coauthor and partner at Smart Advantage, Craig Mowrey, worked tirelessly with me on pulling together the analysis we needed to share these specific stories with you. Craig Mowrey and Brian Neff, another Smart Advantage consultant, were the senior analysts behind the data you will learn about in each of the case studies. Along with me, they have both worked firsthand with many of the clients presented in this book.

Mark Steisel, my other coauthor, somehow maintained his enthusiasm for this project, even while enduring my foibles and frustrations. Mark edited with us endlessly, and did it all with a smile.

I also would like to recognize my good friend, mentor, and cheerleader Ron Fleisher, who encouraged me to press on during times when I felt like this book would never get done. Out of the kindness of his heart, he has taught me a great deal, and has been a guiding force for Smart Advantage.

Pulling this book together also required the help of Ashley Dufrene, who among other tasks, gets credit for creative cover design; and Marie Hope, who assisted in the final stages of publication. Scott Schmidt kept all of us at Smart Advantage on track and inspired me with his unfailing positive attitude, especially when I felt overwhelmed as one can often be when simultaneously writing a book and running a business.

Editors Thomas Hauck and Nathan Denny made sure we crossed our t's and dotted our i's (and, confidentially, ensured us that we made sense!) Both are brilliant editors and I was lucky to have their help.

In Memoriam
William G. Flanagan

Coauthor of my first book, teacher, and friend
Left us February 2010

Bill was both a writer and editor for *The Wall Street Journal*, *Forbes*, *Business Week*, and *Esquire*. He hosted the *Bill Flanagan Show* on WABC radio (a money call in show) and acted as fill in host for Bob Brinker on *Money Talk*. He was a regular on *Lou Dobbs' Money Line* and appeared on *Good Morning America, Today, Fox News,* and other national and local shows.

Introduction

AFTER POLLING THOUSANDS OF CEOs, C-SUITE executives, and salespeople I have been astonished to discover that only a handful knew what their prospects and customers wanted most. This explains in no small measure why so many businesses have become commoditized. Many think that because they sell the same product or service as their competition, they must surrender and play a price game. And when they do, they give up their best negotiation chips.

Prior to the release of my first book, *Creating Competitive Advantage* (Doubleday 2006). I flew all over the globe helping companies identify what differentiated them from their competition (and I still do). The research we conducted for that book proved that over ninety percent of businesses had no clue how to articulate their competitive advantages, and I have since learned that even *fewer* understand that a *differentiator that is not valued by the customer is not a competitive advantage. If it's not relevant, it doesn't matter.*

Relevant Selling is the perfect title for this book. The years of research upon which this book is based revealed that very few businesses deliver sales and marketing pitches that are relevant. And that mistake costs them dearly! Most businesses simply do not align their operations with their customers' priorities—internally or externally. This is not just my opinion or conjecture, but our key findings from more than one hundred customer surveys conducted for our client companies.

Surprisingly, when companies make key internal decisions, very few of them give their customers' perspectives the weight they deserve. Fewer yet use their customers' perspectives to craft their sales and marketing messages, and virtually none have internal agreement regarding what their customers value. Most use a single marketing message regardless of the diverse requirements of their specific target markets, demographics, and levels of customers. More often than not, customers and prospects value different things, but most salespeople deliver the same messages to both. Usually this occurs because they don't know what each group values most.

Creating Competitive Advantage revealed that most businesses want to be alike, not different. Simply look at the websites of your top competitors. Generally speaking, everyone is using the same clichés. For example, I haven't seen one health-care organization—from hospitals and

hospices to home care and assisted-living facilities—
that doesn't position itself as "caring and passionate,"
offering family members "peace of mind." Certainly,
being "caring and passionate" are honorable traits,
but what exactly do those terms actually mean? What
specific information do they convey? When those words
alone are used in marketing, they ring hollow and sound
hackneyed. They're empty words, and worse yet they
have no *relevance*.

Manufacturers all want to tout their customer service
and quality. Service companies want to talk about their
knowledgeable staffs and responsiveness. You get the
picture. Blah, blah, blah. When you use those terms, how
do they show that you're different or better?

HOW RELEVANT SELLING CAME TO BE

Businesspeople who read *Creating Competitive
Advantage* often e-mail me long lists of their newly
identified and neatly "wordsmithed" competitive advantages. They ask me, "What do you think?" My answer
is always the same: "It doesn't matter what I think; it
matters what your customers think."

Ninety percent of the more than three thousand mid-
sized businesses that I've polled confessed that they have
no idea what their customers really value—they only
guess. They have no process or line item expenditures for

scientifically finding what their customers and prospects prize most.

On the other hand, large companies with substantial research budgets invest significantly to collect the voice of the customer, but few use the information effectively. Amazingly, even the large companies in our study rarely knew what their customers valued most.

That revelation was the inspiration for *Relevant Selling*. At Smart Advantage, we have been analyzing customer research findings for our client companies for many years. These companies range from the smallest startups to *Fortune 500* companies and include businesses in manufacturing, service, distribution, and retail. In this book, you'll read about every kind of business imaginable: manufacturers of wine kits, credit cards, and roof tiles; providers of luxury tours, pest control, and insurance; purveyors of fine foods, financial services, and chemicals; distributors of building materials, software, and door knobs; and many more. We cover the gamut.

We tracked the results of all those customer studies and compared them to the companies' perceptions of what their markets valued. Frequently, what company staffs and sales forces thought would be most important was rated lowest by the customers themselves. Ouch!

We found several surprising common denominators in all of the customer studies we analyzed. They can best be described as blind spots that are inherent in virtually every business. They are roadblocks to true competitive advantages. They preclude organizations from avoiding price wars. Even companies that proudly claimed that they "don't engage in price wars" were leaving profits on the table.

Creating Competitive Advantage successfully shows companies how to find and tout their potential competitive advantages. It clearly filled a need for thousands of businesses in the last few years. But the research analysis we conducted made me realize there was a critically important additional level that these businesses needed to reach in order to truly define their competitive advantages. They had to learn whether the attributes that they think are their competitive advantages are, in fact, *relevant* to their customers. We found a frightfully large percentage of companies were way off the mark.

Finding their true competitive advantages means companies have to confirm, beyond a reasonable doubt, which of their differentiators made an impact on their customers' buying decisions. Most businesses brainstorm to come up with a list of their "strengths" or they have their marketing firm do it for them. Then they throw the all the results against the wall and hope some stick. Well, some do. But wouldn't it make more sense to throw them at the bull's-eye and get more direct hits?

WHAT THIS BOOK CONTAINS

Chapter One explains the cost of irrelevance and shows where companies go astray. I explain how and why it's so easy to believe the myth that price is of the greatest importance to buyers. You'll read the first two of many case studies of companies that were misaligned, and what they did about it.

One explanation of how companies fall off track is that they get unreliable customer feedback. Their sources are not always sound, and faulty data can often steer management and sales teams off course. Problems with feedback will be described in Chapter Two.

Chapters Three through Eight break down blind spots we discovered and show how each was handled by companies profiled. Chapters Nine and Ten will "lead you to the well." You'll learn how and where to get the customer information you need and how easy, and often inexpensive, it can be.

Throughout this book you will find actual case studies that support our findings. This will make it easier for you to apply their lessons to your own business. Once the blinders were removed from the companies in our studies and they took action, it made an enormous difference in close rates, margin protection and revenue growth.

We often experience pushback from some company teams: "Customers don't always know what they want." I hear that a lot. And I agree. After all, customers didn't tell Steve Jobs to create the iPhone. When we design survey questions, we don't ask customers what product innovations they want. Instead, we focus on asking customers and prospects what factors most influence their buying decisions. That's what we are discussing in

Relevant Selling. This book is about quantitative evaluations, and the ranking of attributes based on *what and how you sell today.*

My hope is that when you finish reading this book you will come to realize that *relevant selling* has everything to do with defining your company's culture, planning its strategy, and knowing what to measure. Without this knowledge, it's a crap shoot. It can be very costly.

There's a terrific metaphor used by Ram Charan in his book *Execution* (Crown, 2002), written with Larry Bossidy: "Too many leaders fool themselves into thinking their companies are well run. They're like the parents in Garrison Keillor's fictional Lake Wobegon, all of whom think their children are above average."

That's an effective metaphor to describe leadership and execution, and I've become convinced that the same metaphor applies to organizations' views on their knowledge of their customers. Most think that they're in touch, that they know for certain what their customers want, and they're positive they deliver it. Yet nearly every time we deliver to a client their own customers' preferences from research findings, we look squarely into dropped jaws. It gives new meaning to an "Aha!" moment.

ONE LAST THOUGHT

Many companies love to proudly espouse their value propositions. One very large client spent millions with a giant consulting firm writing value propositions that they told us they eventually tossed out. They learned they weren't relevant.

If you do an Internet search to find the meaning of the term "value proposition" you will find many definitions. My favorite is: "A description of the value that your offering will provide to a customer segment, customer or individual that is *relevant, measureable*, and *relative* to their alternative choices." (FutureSight Consulting). If organizations would simply seek to meet this definition, they might qualify for the status of Garrison Keillor's Lake Wobegon children; they might really become above average.

Marketing and sales without serious consideration of what the customer values is flawed. Negotiation without it is impossible. Strategic planning is unsound. By simply giving the customer's perspective the weight it deserves in decision making, internal and external alignment will support relevant selling.

Caution: What is relevant to your customers today isn't likely to be relevant tomorrow. Keep listening and aligning accordingly. The dividends are worth it.

Jaynie L. Smith

CHAPTER 1

Relevant Selling Frees You from Price-Based Negotiation

WHY SHOULD I BUY FROM YOU?

I always ask my client companies that question. Because if you can't reel off relevant answers, your prospects and customers will either demand the lowest price or they will buy from someone else. Businesses that don't - or can't - give relevant differentiators paint themselves into the commodity corner where they're forced to make price the tiebreaker. If you're one of the lucky ones, and price is frequently *not* your tiebreaker, then honing your relevant selling skills will increase your current close rates while further protecting your margins.

In the last ten years we have analyzed double-blind

customer market research for over a hundred companies. We can say, from research, that ninety percent of companies do not adequately "sell" what their customers and prospects want most. Why? Because most companies don't *know* what their customers want most. Sounds preposterous, doesn't it? And yet, in this book, I will show how years of research has proven it true.

First, companies get hung up on selling their product or service, which often has been commoditized. However, their customers are usually looking for "how" those companies sell, not "what" they sell. For example, I can buy doorknobs from scores of suppliers, but if I want my orders to be delivered on time, in full, and accurately, I will seek out the vendor that can meet my demands, and I will be willing to pay more to get what I want. I won't pay more for the doorknob, but I will pay more to get it delivered accurately, in full, when I need it. What good is a cheaper doorknob if it's too late for my production deadline?

Second, way too many companies have no solid basis for how they determine their sales messages. Although most business people believe they know their customers' top buying criteria, the majority are in the dark. Instead, they offer what *they* think their prospects and customers want, not what those prospects and customers *actually* prefer. In other words, their sales messages are irrelevant.

Irrelevant selling is pervasive and its cost to businesses is huge. Our study examined large, small, local, national, and international organizations covering manufacturing, retail, distribution, and service sectors. Companies that took steps to determine what was relevant to their customers and prospects have had compelling success stories. In the pages ahead, you will learn how simple it can be to find what is most relevant to your customers.

Relevance cannot be a part-time discipline. It must be your consistent focus throughout the entire sales process, from the initial marketing materials you use to generate leads, to well after the ink dries on the final receipt! Lack of relevance distorts your aim. It's like shooting at a target with a gun that has a bent sight. You're sure to miss.

If you have a ninety percent close rate, your messages are probably quite relevant. Few companies have that degree of success, though, because most have a significant number of competitors, and many of those rivals are willing to cut their prices in order to gain market share. They still haven't learned that bigger is not always better. Many of the companies we studied are in drastically fragmented markets and their competitors range from small mom-and-pops to giant conglomerates. It's hard to win the price game in that environment, isn't it? When I speak to CEO groups nationally, I always ask them to rank how much competition they have, on a one-to-ten scale (with ten being "lots"). About seventy five percent say eight, nine, or ten – and some even say thirteen or twenty! If that's the case, how can you ever win the price game? Someone will always go lower. You must not only sell value, but more specifically, the value the customer is seeking. Few companies do.

MISTAKEN BELIEFS

When companies survey their prospects and customers to find out what they want most, they learn, time after time, that their prior assumptions are conclusively wrong. In fact, our clients have called the findings of their attribute testing/customer research surveys "jaw dropping," "eye opening," and "game changing." The most common misconception is that price drives sales, but it rarely does. Similarly, the importance of relationships is frequently overrated.

Like nasty viruses, the price and relationship fallacies can cause great harm and be hard to kill. As you might expect, many salespeople initially disagree. They tell me, "My customers buy because of their relationships with me." To some extent, that may be true, but then I ask, "Do you think your competitors have the ability to build and maintain good relationships too? I bet they let their customers win at golf just as often as you do."

When they counter, "That's reality," I ask, "Okay then, what's your tiebreaker? What is the one thing your customers want most from you and are sure that you will deliver?" Invariably, the fallback position is, "A lower price." One client told me that when his salespeople lose a sale, they say it was because of price, but when they win, they claim it was because of their relationship. Can you relate to this?

In all the double-blind studies of buying criteria that we've reviewed, price has rarely been anywhere near the top of the list of what customers really wanted. I've even interviewed five good-sized market research firms that have been analyzing customer research studies decades longer than I have. Each confirmed my observations. When a study is blind (meaning the customer doesn't know who commissioned the study), they found that price most often falls in the bottom quintile of buying criteria. (Blind studies allow the respondent to tell the truth; there's no reason to "negotiate" with the research interviewer.) Sales folks are often convinced that price is the tiebreaker because prospects and customers are always negotiating with them to get a better deal. I'm not naïve enough to say that price is *never* at the top of *some* buyers' lists. But if you and your team can shift your mindset to acknowledge that price doesn't always have to rule, and you begin to sell more relevantly, you might close at least ten to thirty percent more business without giving away any of your precious margin. Imagine what that would do for your close ratios, your sales commissions, and your company's bottom line.

Buyers almost always value a number of attributes more than price. They will gladly pay more because of a seller's *financial stability, customer service response time,* and *on-time deliveries with accurate fill rates,* even when they're buying commodities. And that's just a partial list.

Price comes into play when you neglect to explain, for example, how your customer response record is far better than that of your nearest competitor. Price trumps value if you don't know what value your customers want or how to sell it. If you don't value what you do for your customers, meaning, if you don't *put a value on it*, they won't value it either. In my twenty-four years of consulting with hundreds of businesses, I have been staggered by how few companies sell value really well. Many shamelessly chant the cliché "we sell value," but do little to clearly explain and/or quantify what that means to the customers. Nature abhors a vacuum, and price is often the default value.

Put yourself in your customer's shoes. *Be* your customer!

- "What good is a lower price if my order doesn't get here in time for my production run?"
- "What good is a lower price if I get the wrong parts?"
- "What good is a lower price if I have to call fifteen times to get the order?"
- "What good is a lower price if my supplier goes out of business?"
- "What will it cost me to find another supplier?"
- "What good is a lower price if the widget/gadget/system I ordered doesn't work as promised?"
- "What good is a cheaper general contractor who doesn't show up to manage his subs?"

These are the values you bring to the table, not just a lower price.

Jack Daly, the dynamic sales trainer, coach, and speaker, points out, "There's hardly anything that goes on in a sales call that couldn't be anticipated before your arrival. As such, there's no reason to not be prepared. The best salespeople are 'canned,' meaning they say the same thing, the same way, each time encountered. The key, though, is they don't sound canned, it sounds like the very first time they've said it. They discovered what works!"

To me Jack is saying the best sales people consistently deliver the message *most relevant* to the majority of customers.

SPEAKING OF DOORKNOBS

Martin Wardhaugh is the Division Managing Director of Mila, a group of companies in Europe that develop and distribute door and window hardware (handles, hinges, locks and technical products) to fenestration fabricators (window and door makers).

Mila is clearly selling highly commoditized products: they have over a hundred competitors of all sizes and only a handful of truly unique products. They buy some of their products in China and distribute in the UK, Ireland, Scandinavia, and the Baltics. They first asked us to help them with their UK division.

Daventry, in the beautiful English countryside, is the headquarters of Mila UK. Less than two hours north of London, Daventry began around AD 920 as a small Anglo-Saxon village. Seven hundred years later, the town was mentioned by William Shakespeare in *Henry VI*. Because of high quality transport links, Daventry is now a warehousing and distribution center. North of town is a major terminal for freight interchange between road and railways. This is an ideal location for a company like Mila.

When we first arrived we were given a tour of the facility and were very impressed with the company's internal processes that ensured inventory was well managed and accounted for. Martin, overseeing all of the Mila operations, was very clear on why he wanted to work with us. Because of the intense competition in their business, his sales staff had a deeply held belief that they had to compete on price. After all, as in many businesses, their customers beat them up about price every day. It was a sales mentality Martin desperately wanted to change. At the same time he needed help defining what "value" really meant to his customer, so his people could confidently and justifiably hold the line on their prices. This is a widespread issue for many companies, further exacerbated by the new, lousy economy.

I have already said that less than ten percent of companies we've studied clearly knew what their customers valued most in their buying decisions. Mila was one of the ten percent who *did* know. Their belief that customers wanted *on-time delivery*, *order accuracy*, and *product reliability* was exactly what the market research study confirmed. So we simply asked them, "Since you know what is relevant, please tell us how you sell these attributes today in sales calls."

After a long pregnant pause, followed by a great deal of internal discussion, they confessed, "Not well... not well at all." Even though they knew what was important to the customer, they rarely discussed it in sales calls.

For starters, we challenged them on the most important attribute: "Let's talk about *on-time delivery*. How do you define that?"

One manager said, "We promise next day delivery, so if they order before five in the afternoon we get it out the door that night and they get it the next day."

Another quipped, "Some customers don't want it the next day. They don't want it until they need it."

Yet another, "Some say they want it the next day, but they're used to getting it in the morning because of their position on the delivery truck's route. Then when the driver takes a different route and their delivery is in the afternoon, they perceive it as being late."

Don't be surprised if this sounds familiar; we've had a similar discussion with every client for whom *on-time delivery* is a top attribute.

We then asked, "If an order goes out on time but you didn't have all the line items, is that order going out 'accurately' and 'on time' according to the customers?" These questions were met with expressions ranging from curious to chagrined. Thus began the journey to relevance.

Martin's team became very operationally focused for Mila. They were determined to make sure the customers got what they wanted - full and complete orders and totally reliable products - when they wanted it, ideally 99.9 percent of the time (no one's perfect).

They also became excited by the opportunity to really become a leader in their market. The market research had identified that no one single company was perceived as best when it came to the most relevant attributes.

Several months later Mila was able to arm their sales-people with the following relevant messaging:

- 98.9 percent on-time in-full orders for the last ten months.
- 96.7 percent order accuracy for the last ten months.

The Mila team also knew that *product reliability* was critical to their customers, but had never touted it, except in the more general context of quality (this is not uncommon). Not all the salespeople knew about Mila's reliability testing; those who did, didn't consider it unique enough to brag about in their sales presentations, until the market research results.

Now they can, and do, say:

- All new Mila door products released in the last five

years have been tested to 100,000 operating cycles, twice the industry standard for door hardware.

- Mila's window products are tested to 50,000 cycles; the British standard is only 10,000 cycles.

- No ninety-day guarantees here. Mila's products are all guaranteed for three to five years, and their security products are guaranteed for ten years.

Once the supportive operations were enhanced, we were ready to arm the salespeople. So back across the pond we went, with carefully crafted sales tools identifying for the Mila sales team their competitive advantages that were most relevant to the people who made buying decisions.

I have a master's degree in human relations (counseling) and I know better than to think that we could wave our magic wand and all the salespeople would suddenly accept that these new tools would be the magic panacea that would dissolve all their price issues. Behavior doesn't change overnight. We had a great deal of convincing to do. We, of course, have seen the positive results repeatedly; but like kid learning to ride a bike, they just had to try it themselves.

We engaged them in some role play, and asked how they felt being at the receiving end of this new relevant selling dialogue. Most admitted it sure sounded more like a real value proposition. Almost all of them confessed that they previously focused on the product, the product, and the product in their sales calls. We pointed out that their competition can offer the same product, but Mila was the only one who could prove 98.9 percent delivery on time and in full. They are the only player in their market with a testing lab that tests product life two to five times the industry standards.

Martin has told us that since we started working with them they had managed to effectively implement a price increase on their imported products, while most of their competitors had simply sucked up the increase in inbound purchase costs. Consequently, their gross margins have been preserved and in fact, have nudged slightly upwards. Furthermore, Mila's sales volumes have held steady in a year when the market contracted by a further ten percent.

Within a month of the sales training, one long-serving Mila sales manager used the metrics on delivery performance and accuracy to help conclude a technical dispute with a large and very demanding customer. He used the newly crafted relevant competitive advantage statements to demonstrate that Mila's one late delivery was out of character with the vast majority of products dispatched from Daventry day in and day out.

The big prize for Mila, however, is the market leadership position that they now crave. They have realized that while they were among the ten percent of our clients who correctly guessed what their customers wanted, in all honesty their business was not totally oriented around these needs.

Our work has now been incorporated into a much

larger change management program within Mila's operations. Their goal is to remodel their business processes and ways of working, to truly put the needs of their customers top of mind, all day, every day. This includes changing the resource allocations on quality management to improve product quality, and reducing stocked product range size and complexity to make sure they can concentrate on delivering great service and accurate orders each and every time.

THE BACKDROP

My company has worked with hundreds of different organizations in scores of industries. I also speak annually at scores of CEO roundtables and association events. Since irrelevant selling is such a pervasive problem, I always ask CEOs and C-suite executives who attend how often they solicit the "voice of the customer." At last count, I've posed this question to more than five thousand corporate leaders.

Remarkably, less than ten percent of mid-market companies seek the voice of the customer in a scientifically designed anonymous survey. That's right, less than one out of every ten. They think it's too costly, or they don't know how to ask, or they think they already know their customers' preferences. Some have invested in customer satisfaction surveys, which work well as company "report cards" that tell businesses how well they are doing. But customer satisfaction surveys only test the things a business asks about; they don't reveal what is most important: their prospects' and customers' buying criteria, how those criteria differ from the staff's beliefs, and how the company is perceived vis à vis their competitors.

On the other hand, many large national and international companies shell out big bucks to discover their customers' preferences, yet most, by their own admission, don't connect the dots internally. Many conduct the research, but few use the results to create clearly defined sales, marketing, and strategic initiatives. What a waste! It reminds me of high-priced designer shoes kept in someone's closet and never worn: a big investment with no return. Consequently, businesses of all sizes fail to use their customers' perspectives as roadmaps to help them create relevant sales and marketing messages, make responsible and accurate resource allocations, and plan for the future. I call this a lost discipline – a very costly lost discipline.

Since the publication of my first book, *Creating Competitive Advantage,* I've received countless e-mails from readers and from those who have attended my presentations. Many realized the enormous power that competitive advantages could offer their companies, so they diligently compiled lists of those potential competitive advantages and proudly sent them to me. Some even went further: they rushed to insert their newly articulated "competitive advantages" into brochures, websites, and sales presentations.

When I receive these lists, I always ask, "That's a great list, but how do you know which of the twelve items you listed, if any, are most valued by your customers? Which are relevant in their buying decisions?"

A look of consternation appears, and they reply, "Well, I guess it's this one."

The key word is *guess*. Believe it or not, most companies – the ninety percent we talked about earlier – are just guessing. They're rolling the dice and the odds are certainly not in their favor. Heck, I know little or nothing about shooting craps, but even I can win once in awhile. In business, "once in a while" is not a good strategy. By guessing, you're jeopardizing your sales and marketing messages, and thus, your bottom line.

So what comes next? Generally, a plea for a lower price or an attempt to turn on the Hugh Grant or Ms. Congeniality charm in hopes of reinforcing the "relationship."

Kudos to these companies who have worked at articulating their potential competitive advantages; their messaging is very likely better than it was, because it replaced vague generalities, cliché's, and empty promises. But what they have really done is articulate their differentiators. Reminder – differentiators that are not *relevant* are not competitive advantages.

LONG HELD BELIEFS

Let me tell you about a wonderful business that found out exactly how far from relevance it had strayed, and what its switch to relevant selling accomplished.

Big Five Tours & Expeditions is a dynamic, high-end adventure tour operator. They package and wholesale trips that travel agents sell to travelers looking for dream vacations and excursions. Big Five offers all sorts of exotic tours including once-in-a-lifetime customized African safaris, Galapagos Islands explorations, Egyptian ruins tours, and Antarctic cruises.

I had the pleasure of traveling with Big Five on a spectacular trip to Machu Picchu in Peru, a destination that had long been on my "bucket list." My trip occurred after Big Five became conscious of relevant selling, and my fellow travelers and I were the lucky recipients of what the company had learned just months before.

Big Five has always invested in producing beautiful brochures loaded with prize-winning photography that give travelers a sense of the amazing tours they can take. The company distributes these brochures to travel agents who, in turn, give them to travelers who may be interested in taking adventure trips. In their marketing and sales messages, Big Five repeatedly emphasized that travel agents should sell their trips to their traveler clients because Big Five was consistently ranked in the top of *Travel + Leisure* Magazine's list of award-winning tour operators. Even the famed *National Geographic*

Adventure magazine bestowed awards on Big Five for their exceptional tours. Big Five's staff thought that relevant selling and marketing meant touting that the tour packager was an award-winning family business that had been around for more than thirty years. Their sales message was off the mark by a mile, and had been for years.

CEO and founder Mahen Sanghrajka is a socially conscious, warm, and fun-loving gentleman of Indian descent who was born in Kenya. About five years ago, his son, Ashish, who had worked in the brokerage business with Charles Schwab, brought his skills to help grow the family business. Ashish now serves as the company president. Big Five was very successful for many years, and then along came the dreaded recession.

Mahen and Ashish had read *Creating Competitive Advantage* and wanted to identify and capitalize on the company's competitive advantages. However, like so many other companies, they had difficulty seeing the forest for the trees.

When they embarked upon our process, the Big Five team committed themselves to soliciting the voice of their customers. The sales and management people identified some fifty-eight possible competitive advantages. We needed to identify Big Five's potential competitive advantages in order to test which, if any, truly mattered to travel agents. We also needed to determine what travelers valued most when they chose a tour operator to deliver their travel services. So Big Five commissioned two double-blind customer research surveys: one of travel agencies, and the other of travelers.

Let me briefly digress to tell you a little about surveys. We recommend that our clients invest in double-blind customer research surveys because these provide the most reliability and objectivity. In double-blind surveys, neither the interviewer nor the respondent knows who has sponsored the survey. I also want to point out that when we work with clients, we do not conduct their customer research surveys. We help design the survey to ensure that the best questions are asked, but our clients hire a separate, independent professional research company to conduct the interviews and compile the results. We then analyze and interpret those results.

Back to Big Five. They were stunned by the survey results. We tested twenty possible items, or "attributes," that could be paramount in the buying decisions of travel agents and travelers. The big surprise was that the travel agents rated *travel awards* dead last in their buying criteria, out of twenty the attributes tested. The travelers? They rated the travel awards attribute next to last. Plus, no one cared about *longevity*. Oops! Big Five was definitely *not* selling relevantly.

In upcoming chapters, I'll give you more details on Big Five, and how the company ultimately addressed relevant selling. But for now, let me tell you that during the recession, when many of their peers disappeared or limped along, learning what was relevant saved the company. In fact, Big Five's sales have been up some forty percent year over year.

OPTIONS

Would you return to an award-winning restaurant if you didn't like the food? You might if you had no other choice – but buyers usually have plenty of choices, and sooner or later they will pay for what they want.

Do you know what your customers actually want? Chances are you'll say, "Heck, yes."

Keep the following in mind. We have tested more than two thousand of our clients' employees, and only a handful correctly guessed what their prospects and customers actually valued most. For some, the question felt like a *Jeopardy* Final Question – they bet an awful lot on a guess.

Failure to obtain and use the customers' perspective is epidemic and the cost is staggering. I think we could jump-start the economy and breathe life into many companies that are coasting at or below the red line if more of them simply focused on relevant selling. Imagine if every company in the US could earn just ten percent more revenues! The cash pump would start working again.

MY BIG QUESTION

When I first discovered how many businesses could not identify their customers' most important preferences, it shocked me. I kept asking myself, "Why are so many companies unclear about what their customers value the most?" Since their success depends on satisfying their customers, I couldn't understand why they didn't know precisely what their customers truly want – especially since it's so easy to learn.

I began to look for the reasons. I was mystified and needed to understand why so many smart, successful companies were not maximizing their profits. I questioned my clients, the CEOs, and the business people I met. Were they just too busy or did they simply not know that a blueprint is available that would enable them to increase their profits?

Here's what I found. Even the most profitable companies are often not as relevant as they might be, and they frequently fail to raise the earnings bar as high as they could, for the following reasons:

- **Unreliable or biased sources.** Some of the feedback that businesses rely on is out of date. Remember, although soliciting the voice of the customer provides the most reliable feedback, few companies solicit essential information in a disciplined, scientific manner on a regular basis. And even those who do, frequently fail to use that data well.

A specialty grocery retailer was preparing to invest an online ordering system for their customers because their employees suggested it. The suggestion was based on the employees' instincts and opinions. When surveyed, the company's customers rated online ordering dead last in what they wanted from a specialty grocer. Most of us want to pick out our own peaches and personally eyeball the meat we plan to prepare.

- **Diverse internal perspectives.** When executives and sales teams were asked what they thought mattered most to their prospects and customers, ninety-five percent of the team members had very different perspectives. Title and/or function in the company commonly colored each person's perspective. Ask your team what they think your customers want most. I will put all my chips on the table and make this prediction: no three members of your management team will agree on what they think are your prospects' and customers' top three buying criteria. I've repeatedly seen salespeople say, *post-sales support* and/or *knowledge of sales reps* are the most important items their customers value. Yet in many company surveys, these items barely make the halfway mark. Customer Service thinks the most important element is *customer support*; Human Resources thinks it's *personnel qualifications*; IT is convinced it's the bells and whistles of *technology*. People are usually biased in favor of what they personally deliver. Their opinions are based on *their* perspectives, not customers' perspectives.

- **Corporate investments and strategic disciplines are not related to customers' top buying criteria.** About ninety percent of companies we studied did not align their planning with their customers' most important buying criteria. So it's hard to sell relevance when internally a team's actions do not support what customers want the most.

A major food supplier sells to distributors. The distributors then sell the supplier's goods to restaurant chains and independent owners who, in turn, sell them to end users (the dining public). Since the distributors are first-level customers and big influencers, the supplier assumed that distributors' main concern was price, which would drive *their* profit margin. Their real wake-up call was when they learned that, first and foremost, their distributors wanted their food supplier to make *accurate, on-time deliveries*. Late or inaccurate deliveries force distributors to waste their valuable time sorting out issues instead of selling more products.

- **Prospects and customers buy for different reasons.** So do different levels of customers, such as influencers and decision makers. However, many companies deliver the same sales messages to all. Our research found that about seventy percent of the time, what was most relevant to existing customers differed from what was most relevant to prospects. The studies also revealed frequent disparities between what decision makers and influencers valued most.

The Institute for Trend Research (ITR) discovered that their existing customers prized *on-time delivery* of data more than prospects did; prospects had not yet come to rely on the data enough to value its timeliness. But ITR's prospects valued *frequency of communication* with the company more than did existing clients. ITR's customers had come to realize that they didn't need additional communication. Prospects, unfamiliar with ITR's work, wanted assurances that their data supplier would be available when they needed help.

- **Communication gaps regarding what is truly relevant create operational issues that may preclude relevant selling.** Many companies make little effort to ensure that their employees know how the work they perform relates to customers' buying criteria. Employees who deliver what is most relevant aren't always informed about the role their work plays in delivering the company's value proposition.

A credit union learned that their customers' number one priority was *information security*, which their staff rated just twelfth on a list of items thought to be customers' preferences. So the IT folks who handled data security had to be keenly aware of how much impact their jobs had on the credit union's relevance to their customers. IT employees were mission critical, and they didn't know it.

- **Companies *guess* what is relevant.** Earlier I mentioned that our research found that ninety percent of companies don't actually know what their customers are looking for when they make their buying decision. Big Five was selling the fact that they won awards when neither travel agents nor travelers valued a tour operator's awards highly. A food-service company touted the recipes they provided to customers, only to learn the recipes were not valued highly by the restaurant owners and chefs.

- **The return on investment yielded by investing in disciplined customer research is underestimated.** In the case studies in this book, we will show you how much ROI companies gained. We have seen revenues increase as much as 117 percent for companies that became relevant because of their investment in testing potential competitive advantages. Obtaining the voice of your customer is easier than you think. I will show you how to become a relevant selling organization.

This book will also discuss each of these points based on research we analyzed over the last ten years. We will delve more deeply into case studies of actual companies like Mila and Big Five that went through these eye-opening experiences. The examples that fill this book are not exceptions to the rule, they *are* the rule. As you read on, you'll see many similar stories. Beware! You may be looking in the mirror.

RELEVANT MARKETING / ADVERTISING

When companies pinpoint customers' top buying criteria, their sales and marketing message become more relevant.

An executive of a pest control company showed me an ad his company was about to place in Yellow Page directories. The ad emphasized the safety of the chemicals the company used.

When I asked him how much the ad would cost, he told me, "Roughly $150,000, plus another $100,000 for the same ad in local newspapers, on radio, and TV."

"That's great," I said. "But is the safety of your chemicals your customers' number one buying criterion?

- Does it outweigh getting the bugs dead?
- Isn't the use of safe chemicals now a given in your industry?
- Is the safety of the chemicals you use more important than the fact that your people always show up on time?
- How highly do customers value background checks on the technicians who will be entering their homes?"

When the executive admitted that he didn't know, I replied, "So you're ready to invest a quarter million dollars on ads based on what you *guess* is most important? You may be right, but why risk all your chips on that guess when you can dramatically improve your odds?"

The company's ads now focus on what's most relevant to their customers. As a result, their qualified sales leads are up by about twenty percent. It staggers the mind to think how much money is invested in advertising based on a guess, a whim, or creative design rather than relevance.

WHAT'S AT STAKE

Irrelevant selling causes enormous losses. As Mark Rodgers writes in *Accelerate the Sale* (McGraw-Hill, 2011), only sixteen percent of all salespeople come within ninety percent of their quotas, and a staggering eighty-six percent don't cash in on opportunities because they ask the wrong questions. What if you didn't have to worry about asking the wrong questions? What if, like a magician, you already knew which cards to play? What if you knew that the odds were in your favor, and that you would be relevant in ninety percent of your sales pitches based on a statistically valid study – a study that showed you the top of the bell curve, what most of your customers were seeking? And what if you knew precisely how to speak about those things? Well you can! The companies in this book have learned how. Keep reading and you will too.

FIND OUT HOW CLOSE YOUR COMPANY IS TO RELEVANT SELLING TODAY

Look at your last planning session. Whether it was formal or informal, what were the key objectives your company decided upon? How did those decisions come to be made? What input did you have from customers to determine if your next moves would be relevant?

- Ask your salespeople to rate on a one-to-ten scale how important they think price is in their transactions.
- If you are in sales, and you have to remove price from the buying criteria, what would be next? (I refer to "P R I C E" as the five-letter dirty word in sales.)
- What else do you convey in your sales and marketing efforts that justifies your charging a higher price? Are your differentiators relevant? How do you know?

Determine if you and the rest of your company are very clear on your value proposition. How do you sell a relevant proposition today? Remember, if you don't communicate to your customers how much value you give them, they won't value it.

CHAPTER 2

Relevant Selling Depends on Unbiased Information

MOST OF US ARE FAMILIAR WITH THE CHILDREN'S game "Telephone." Telephone begins when one child whispers a brief message to a friend, who in turn, whispers the same short message to another friend. The sequence continues child by child, until everyone in the group has heard and passed on the message. The result is always the same: when the last child recites the message, it has morphed into something vastly different than what was originally said.

When businesses get feedback from their customers, they often play telephone. Here's how it works. A salesperson questions his or her customer and the customer responds. Then the salesperson tells the district sales manager his or her recollection of what the customer said. The district sales manager then relays the feedback to the regional sales chief. At each rung of the corporate ladder, the feedback, or a version of it, is repeated. Eventually, it reaches a corporate vice president or even the CEO.

Like rivers, feedback usually takes meandering routes. As it flows from person to person, it picks up silt and debris. Each time feedback is repeated, it includes different words, expressions, and meanings. Some information is omitted and it is subject to differing interpretations. As feedback is passed on, it's filtered, rephrased, and changed because each person adds, embroiders, deletes, or downplays certain slants, biases, interests, and perspectives. Add to that our genuinely faulty memories.

People's backgrounds and interests also color feedback. For example, when someone with an manufacturing background receives feedback from a customer about a product, he or she will instinctively focus on how well the item works. Then when that person discusses the feedback with others in the company, he or she may think about the product's mechanics, how it works, sprinkle in some engineering terms, and completely overlook the customer's opinion about the accompanying service that the company provided. Not intentionally, but because that person isn't inclined to think in terms of service because manufacturing is his or her role, and passion. In turn, the next narrator may restate the information, but leave out or misstate the engineering terms, which could cause substantial change.

The result? Decisions made on the basis of internal feedback chains can be flawed and costly.

BIASED INPUT

In addition to getting muddled information, companies don't always get all the facts, including those that may be very important. The leaders of Denholtz Associates, a large commercial real estate developer that leases its properties through independent brokers, prided themselves on being tenant oriented. So they focused on location and invested heavily in the quality and appearance of their properties. However, when they surveyed potential tenants to learn what they wanted most, they found that the top priority was *level of security of the property*: eighty-eight out of a hundred ranked that attribute as number one. The second priority (favored by eighty-six percent of respondents) was *speed of response to tenant issues and/or requests*, with *quality of property maintenance* as a close third.

These survey results set the Denholtz team back on their respective heels. When the brokers who leased the properties provided feedback to the developer, they usually described situations that were important to them and affected their incomes: length of contracts, lease amounts, concessions, and incentives such as improvements and build-outs.

Although many potential tenants asked the brokers about the properties' security, responsiveness to issues, and maintenance, the brokers neglected to tell the developer how frequently these questions were posed. Often in such cases, salespeople are so focused on their own perspective that other issues are often swept aside or given a cursory response. The upshot was that critical questions on security, responsiveness, and maintenance never made their way to the folks making resource allocation decisions. Additionally, the brokers were not selling what was relevant to Denholtz's prospects.

For starters, we recommended that they install new and better lighting and cameras in the properties' parking areas, hire more security personnel, and upgrade their alarm systems.

CEO Steven Denholtz proudly informed me they went beyond our recommendations. He said, "Our changes are much more exciting." Denholtz invested in a centralized system with a call center for all of their properties. So instead of tenants having to contact a property manager or building engineer, they simply log in a work order, and within ten minutes the order is on its way to being addressed. This system can track all security issues for all properties across the region. It also gives the Denholtz team measurements and accountability that allow them to tout their superior management of security, issue resolution, and maintenance requests. Since installing this system, which addressed the top three most desired attributes of their tenants, Denholtz properties are at ninety percent occupancy, and lease renewal rates are up to 88 percent from 70 percent. Steven also reported that his staff has had a real internal surge of positive energy as an added result.

If Denholtz and his team had relied on the information, or lack of information, from brokers and sometimes leasing agents, they never would have learned what tenants valued most. Nor would they have been able to address them effectively, as they ultimately did.

LEND ME YOUR EAR, THEN YOUR MONEY

BDC Capital is the oldest business development corporation in the United States. The company's affiliate, CDC New England (CDC NE), is certified to make government-secured SBA 504 loans to small businesses to finance the acquisition, expansion, or modernization of fixed assets such as real estate or equipment. When small business operators go to banks for SBA 504 loans, the banks' loan officers refer them to companies such as CDC NE to underwrite part of the loan.

CDC NE's management team thought that much of their business was based on *relationships* and the *good-old-boy network*. To get referrals, the company's salespeople called on loan officers and tried to forge relationships with them. They played golf with the officers, took them to dinner, invited them to parties, and established personal relationships with them. At the end of the day, the loan officers ate heartily, lowered their handicaps, and enjoyed the perks – but when they needed mortgages processed quickly, they often called CDC NE's competitors.

When CDC NE commissioned a double-blind customer survey, they discovered the cold, hard truth: when loan officers made referrals to lenders, *relationships* were not foremost on their minds. Instead, their top four priorities were items that management had not considered crucially important:

1. *Speed of response*
2. *Problem solving*
3. *Communication*
4. *Accessibility*

"Obviously, our investments and strategic disciplines were not aligned with our customers' buying criteria," said Kenneth J. Smith, BDC's President and CEO. "We were doing it wrong."

Salespeople frequently project their perspectives on their customers: they assume that their customers want what they want. For example, a number of our clients are wholesalers that sell products to retailers. When we asked some wholesalers' sales staffs what they thought retailers considered most important, they ranked *reputation* and *level of support by sales reps* at the top.

Yet when customers were surveyed, they rated level of *support by sales reps* near the bottom of the attributes tested, and *reputation* rarely made the top five. Although support by sales reps and reputation is important to salespeople, buyers don't always consider those attributes to be very important.

The bottom line is this: it is risky to assume that your salespeople are the best or most reliable sources of feedback. Their primary job is to sell, not to gather feedback. So when you rely on them to learn what your customers' value the most, through no fault of their own the information you receive may be flawed. And if you create sales messages based on faulty feedback or untested opinion, those messages will likely be irrelevant and costly.

HEARSAY IS NOT RELEVANT

We came face to face with the unreliability of feedback from some salespeople with LaSalle Bristol, LP (LSB). The company is headquartered in Elkhart, Indiana, a railway center about midway between Chicago and Toledo. Elkhart prides itself on being a friendly, hometown community in the heart of Amish Country. It's the RV capital of the world and the birthplace of Alka-Seltzer.

LSB manufactures and supplies a wide range of products to builders of factory-built homes, modular homes, and recreational vehicles. The company sells plumbing parts such as pipes, fittings, tubs, and showers, as well as flooring, lights, fans, tile, siding, and furniture. LSB does not sell electrical parts, while some of their competitors sell both plumbing and electrical supplies. But LSB is the market leader in the products they supply.

The company's salespeople felt they were losing sales opportunities because the company didn't offer bundled packages of electrical and plumbing parts. In fact, when we asked them to list what they thought their customers wanted most, they ranked the *ability to offer bundled products such as plumbing and electrical* sixth out of twenty-three attributes. Two executives ranked bundling in the top three: a product category vice president and a general manager.

So we designed a survey to find out what LSB's customers actually valued most. Among other questions the survey specifically asked, "Do you purchase your plumbing product from the same vendor that you purchase your electrical products?" Here's what the survey revealed:

- The majority, thirty-two out of fifty respondents, answered, "None of the time."
- Only three of those questioned said, "All the time."
- The remaining fifteen replied, "Some of the time."

In a follow-up question, the survey asked respondents to rank the importance of the ability to offer bundled products such as plumbing and electrical. They placed it twentieth among twenty-three attributes listed. Finally, when customers were asked for a wish list of what they would like from a supplier, they named thirty items, but bundling was not one of them.

The survey conclusively showed a statistically significant difference between the feedback from some of LSB's salespeople and what LSB's customers and prospects said they actually wanted. Frequently, the reason this type of discrepancy occurs is because salespeople rely on what I call "a survey of one." When a salesperson acts on the opinion of just one or two customers, that opinion may not reflect the beliefs of a statistically valid representation of all customers; that's a survey of one. Organizations often get burned when they rely on feedback based on surveys of one.

When we met with LSB's staff, we were struck by the fact that the majority had been with the company for decades. By and large, they were conservative and traditionally oriented. We were concerned that they would be so entrenched in their ways that they would reject our approach. Boy, were we wrong! Except for a single skeptic, they loved what we said and wholeheartedly embraced our recommendations, which they perceived as powerful new tools that would steer LSB out of the old ways, keep them from growing stale, and propel them forward.

The lone skeptic was adamant and vocal. He insisted that sales were built on relationships, not competitive advantages or relevance. He argued that the secret of LSB's success was the longstanding, close customer relationships that the sales force had painstakingly built.

Rick Karcher, LSB's President and CEO, was our staunchest supporter. He knew that LSB could not survive by relying on price and relationships. In the past, management viewed LSB as a parts supplier, so price and relationships were the keys to sales. But now, Rick understood, LSB had to be more than a parts supplier. In today's global economy LSB faces heavy competition, so the company needs to become a service organization. LSB had to learn what was most relevant to their customers so the company could promptly fill those customers' needs.

Shortly after LSB followed our recommendation to quantify their competitive advantages, their key sales people delivered a presentation. When the prospect was told that LSB had a 98.6 percent on-time delivery rate, the prospect shrugged it off as if it were no big deal. But a week later, one of LSB's competitors told the same prospect that his company had a 96.1 percent on time delivery rate, and the purchasing agent said, "Oh, yeah, but LSB has a rate of 98.6 percent."

A couple of months after that, a large customer said that it was tired of hearing about LSB's 98.6 percent on-time delivery rate, and complained about the 1.4 percent that was not on time. "So we brought them to our office to spend time with our service team," Rick explains. "We went through all the data, the customers' ordering patterns, and all the steps we have to go through to make sure that we have the right products in stock for them and deliver them on time.

We explained how we measure on-time delivery, and how our employees are accountable for maintaining our high standards. When they came out of that meeting, the 1.4 percent was not an issue. The customer had had a complete change of mind and a new appreciation of how well we served them. Although it didn't win us any new business, it protected quite a bit of business for us."

Quantifying your relevant differentiators makes them more impressive. Even though it may not seem to impress people at first, this is important information that prospects and customers usually don't forget. You never know what people will remember and what facts will stick.

Rick also realized that if LSB's customers wanted on-time delivery, LSB had to focus on providing it. Not just the sales force, but also the entire organization. LSB would have to build a culture dedicated to providing the highest level of service that their customers could ever want. Learning the reasons why LSB's customers bought, Rick believed, gave him a blueprint on where to focus and where to invest.

LSB's sales force now talks a lot about service performance with customers. "The thought process is working its way through the organization, and has been adopted faster by a greater portion of the salespeople than I would have expected," Rick notes.

About a month after LSB began communicating its

relevant messages, the company landed an $800,00 contract with a prospect they had been wooing for years, and were looking to close another $300,000 with that same client. "We clearly won that business because of the relevant selling principles that our sales rep applied," Rick points out. "The interesting thing for me was that price really never came up until late in the conversation, and then it was almost an afterthought." When that sale closed, even the sole skeptic finally started to come around.

THE PRICE MYTH

Each year, I speak to hundreds of CEOs at Vistage roundtables, industry associations, entrepreneurs' organizations, and the like. I always ask the members of the audience to finish this sentence, "My salespeople all tell me they could sell more if only I would ...."

If it weren't so tragic, the answer would be comical because it's always the same. Invariably, those in the audience don't miss a beat. Almost instantly they shout out in unison, "If I would just lower the price."

I follow up that question by asking the CEOs, "Aren't you sick of always hearing that answer?" And they reply with long, resounding groans, "Yes!" I run into the price myth all the time and I love to debunk it. Let me tell you about a few more of our experiences.

For more than seventy years, Driv-Lok® has

engineered fastening solutions for a wide spectrum of industries. They manufacture a number of products including press-fit fasteners, tubular spring pins, machine keys, solid and hollow precision dowel pins, barbed and ferrol studs for use with plastics and composites, knurled pins, and grooved pins. Driv-Lok® also agreed to add the customer research survey as part of our process so that we could identify what their customers valued most. We came up with a list of fifteen service and product items that might rank high. Then we asked distributors, who carried their fasteners, and Original Equipment Manufacturers (OEMs) that used fasteners, what they valued the most, and how Driv-Lok® performed relevant to what they valued. Less than a third of the respondents mentioned price as an important criterion.

With the results of that survey, and at our recommendation, Driv-Lok® clearly identified value propositions for these two distinctly different groups of customers. In the process, company leaders emphasized the attributes that their customers said they wanted most: the ability to (1) *quote immediately and deliver on time* to their distributor customers and (2) provide significant economic improvements/advantages to their OEM customers through their fast, nearly flawless production and delivery systems after *re-engineering the customer's applications* through Driv-Lok®'s EngiNomics® program. This led to their ability to market, price, and deliver strategically to customers in ways that are the most valuable to them, and the most profitable to Driv-Lok®.

FLOWERS AND TLC

Armellini Express Lines, Inc. had a similar experience. Created by a Navy vet and his wife after World War II, this innovative, family-owned delivery service picks up flowers that are air freighted to Miami International Airport and delivers them to wholesalers and mass markets throughout the United States. Armellini, which has a similar operation in Southern California, was the first trucker to offer "flower-specific" refrigeration units for their trailers and the first to use wooden decking that puts less pressure on flower boxes and increases air circulation. Armellini was also one of the first carriers to use satellite tracking to pinpoint the location of their 150 trucks.

Armellini was clearly a market leader in their space, by far the best option in the industry. As a result they were able to command higher price levels than their competition. Then along came the recession. Like so many other companies, Armellini began to feel price pressure. They needed some confidence to hold steady with their pricing to avoid destroying margins like many of their competitors did.

The company's salespeople reported that their prospects and customers would get a price quote from

Armellini's competitors and then demand that Armellini match the hefty discounts that the rivals supposedly offered. So Armellini's salespeople began asking management to lower their prices.

These salespeople didn't doubt that they had the best option for their customers, but they had not been able to articulate their relevant competitive advantages that justified Armellini's premium prices. Like so many companies, they began to take their own superior status for granted. Management began to wonder if the feedback they were getting from customers via their salespeople was a real or an imaginary threat to their market share.

Our challenge was to determine if price was, in fact, the tiebreaker for customers and prospects, or whether they had more important demands. Instead of relying on hearsay and what I like to call negotiation speak – "it's all about price" – Armellini agreed to use a double-blind survey to confirm or deny whether they had to lower their prices in order to survive.

The results of the survey gave them the ammunition they needed not only to hold their price levels but even to raise them slightly. It gave the sales force a renewed sense of confidence that the services Armellini provided were clearly worth more.

When we asked the Armellini executive team to guess how their customers would respond to the survey, they got three of the customers' top four requirements right and got them in the correct order. The feedback they got from their sales force led to their one mistake:

thinking that *price* would be in the top three attributes, which it wasn't. We don't usually include price as one of the attributes tested because our interest is in finding out what customers and prospects value as differentiators. But because Armellini had taken such a beating on price, we made an exception and agreed to include it. As we suspected (but they didn't), price didn't even make the top five. It ranked sixth of the nineteen attributes tested for shippers, and sixth of twenty for wholesalers. *On-time delivery*, *accurate delivery*, *handling of boxes*, *ability to guarantee temperature control*, *quick recovery from a truck breakdown*, and even *billing accuracy* were more important.

"Now, when customers approach us about price, we say, 'Look, we charge what we charge and these are the reasons we charge it,'" CEO David Armellini explains. "Then we show them the bullet points in our sales materials and describe the relevant advantages we bring to the table.

"We've certainly said 'no' to a lot of those who want a lower price and even though we've held our price line, we've retained most of our customers. Since we've held firm on our prices, we've seen about a two-and-a-half percent increase. In a declining market, we've been able to have the confidence to take a rate increase." As I mentioned, our research design doesn't usually test *price* in a list of attributes, but we do offer respondents two or three other ways to highlight price if it is important to them. We start by asking "When you look for a supplier of such and such product or service, what is most important to you?"

When we ask these open-ended questions, it gives respondents the opportunity to say *price* right up front, but few do. Later on, before we conclude the interview, we ask, "What else is important that we did not ask you about?" On average, only twenty to thirty percent mention price, and they do not say that it is "most important." The Armellini staff thought *price* would be one of the top three attributes; it was not.

When we provided Armellini the list of attributes we tested with their wholesalers, aggregately they did guess correctly what the top two attributes were. But the company's messages simply did not convey how they excelled at fulfilling these very specific demands. The next step was to change their marketing and sales messages.

An example of Armellini's current, hard-hitting messaging appears below. Notice that it doesn't mention their charges or fees, or attempt to compete on price. But it does focus on the things that, in most cases, only Armellini offers, and has for years. These are powerful competitive advantages because they are *relevant* to their buyers.

On-time Delivery:
- Armellini is the only transporter to provide ETA on line.
- Last year our 24/7 dispatchers handled 1,800 live calls after hours.

- On-time deliveries tracked at 96.2 percent last 12 months.

Accurate Delivery:
- Only Florida-based transporter to scan every incoming and outgoing box last 22 years.
- Average less than one box short for every 2,500 boxes delivered.

Reliable Temperature control:
- 20 percent more insulation than industry average.
- One of the first to offer continuous airflow, for less than one degree variance.
- 120 outbound loading docks, all temperature controlled and sealed to maintain box temperature.

What makes these competitive advantages powerful is that they speak directly to what buyers want most. Getting the right message was dependent on confirming what the customers really wanted and not accepting all the chatter about price as the final word. If you take customers' negotiation pleas as gospel, you are sure to lose margins.

OTHER FEEDBACK OBSTACLES

Feedback may be unreliable for other reasons. Customers don't always say what they mean. It's not uncommon for them to hold back or soften what they actually feel. Some may not want to hurt salespeople with who they have relationships and genuinely like. We all know the story: they loved us right up until they left us.

To be politically correct, some customers may whitewash their critiques and frame them in less harsh, and less truthful, language. Others may keep quiet or not be totally honest because they don't want to get involved, make waves, or go out on a limb. Think about your own experience. The last time someone asked you to give a reference for a former employee, did you tell it like it was, or did you dress it up somewhat? I have been in restaurants with people who complain to me nonstop about their meals, but when their waiters ask, "How's everything?" they smile and say, "Fine, thanks." Customers of all kinds frequently don't say what they actually feel.

When it comes to reliable feedback, canned customer surveys and generic internet customer surveys may also fall short. The main problem with these surveys is that they're often based on templates that don't fit all situations, and therefore don't provide essential information. Many organizations mistakenly think that if they conduct a customer satisfaction survey, it will put them in touch with the voice of the customer and give them solid and reliable data.

Sadly, it probably won't. Although customer satisfaction surveys are good performance evaluations that generally provide broad-based feedback, they don't reveal what customers want most.

SOCIAL NETWORKS

Social networks and on-line communities have become major sources of feedback because their members tend to accept what fellow network members endorse. And the impact of social media will only grow. Facebook, Twitter, and other social networks are now a central part of millions of people's lives, especially the Y generation – the "Millennials." As they move into the work force and take on larger roles, they will bring their social networking skills with them and make them a part of their businesses.

Feedback races through social media and has an enormous reach. Almost instantaneously, it can reach people in every corner of the earth. Complimentary buzz about a company's goods or services can quickly go viral and propel little-known businesses to international rock-star status. Groupon and Justin Bieber come to mind.

On the flip side, social networks can also be breeding grounds for unreliable feedback. Self-promoting businesses can post questionable information on social networks and have their friends and associates give them the highest praise. Conversely, their rivals can easily post damning indictments, which may not even be true. Comments on social networks aren't required to be factual, and can be based on rumors, misinformation, guesses, impressions, and dubious motives such as the desire for retribution.

Businesses are now capitalizing on the power of

online communities. According to the market research firm Toluna, companies are now creating online communities where they can "interact with one another in real time, online, in a social atmosphere." Listening to on-site chatter, Toluna believes, will enable companies to obtain valuable data and incorporate customer feedback into their marketing approaches. So Toluna is conducting webinars to help companies build information-gathering communities.

By tracking key words on the internet, including on social media sites, companies are learning what customers are saying about their goods and services. Customer chatter is being mined and used as feedback to strengthen their operations and make their messages more relevant.

But some caution should be used before relying on chatter. Often, chatter can be "me too" data that simply repeats what someone said and may not reflect original thoughts, opinions, or the degree of the speaker's knowledge, experience, or conviction.

In other words, it may not deserve much weight. Despite this danger, though, the tracking of internet chatter is very quickly emerging as a potentially powerful customer feedback tool.

When you rely solely on your sales force, generic online surveys, and other do-it-yourself tools, watch out! The risk is high. The information you receive may not be reliable or relevant. It could steer you in the wrong direction. Obtaining customer feedback is an art that involves

numerous subtleties and nuances. It's a highly specialized process that, when done properly by skilled and
experienced professionals, can zero in on precisely what
your customers value and how what they want should be
delivered to them.

DISTINGUISH OPINION FROM FACT

How organizations gather customer input, especially on what customers value most, and how they use that information, has everything to do with their growth rates and profitability. Yet too few companies fully understand and/or act on acquiring this blueprint for planning and relevant selling.

- What methodologies does your company currently employ to gain the voice of the customer, and how does that information make it to the "front line," e.g., the sales force and customer service folks?
- Pull your management team together and ask them how they get feedback. Specifically, find out whom they ask to get feedback, and whether they tell them what information to collect and what questions to ask. Get the names and positions of the people they question and the channels the feedback takes before it reaches them. Learn how many intermediaries are involved and who they are. Then note how far the feedback you receive is from the source. Ask your team members what they do to corroborate and verify the feedback they receive. Compare their answers. Look for similarities in votes and find the discrepancies.
- What kinds of surprises has your company had when you lost a prospect, because you didn't know what was most important to them, and you missed

talking about it? How was the feedback from that loss conveyed to the rest of your organization?

- If you haven't invested in formal market research, then ask salespeople how they get feedback and how often they get it. How high a priority is getting feedback from them? Identify the people they speak to in order to get feedback and how they record the information they receive. Do they take notes or record their conversations at the time they receive feedback, or do they try to write it up later "from memory?" Find out how many sources they use and what they do to corroborate and verify the information they receive. Also ask to whom they give the feedback they get. Do they insert it into your CRM? Does Sales Management compare feedback from multiple sources and look for common themes?

- Make gathering feedback a high priority, so that you receive it at least every few months. Create a system to gather and verify feedback and to hold people accountable for getting and authenticating it. List the information you wish to get and write the questions to be asked. Clarify how all information will be communicated and to whom. Create verification standards so when you factor feedback in your decisions, you will be able to decide how much you can rely on it.

CHAPTER 3

Guesswork Undermines Relevant Selling

90% of Companies Guess at What's Relevant

I DO CROSSWORD PUZZLES. IT MAKES ME CRAZY WHEN I can't think of something I know I should know. That's how the teams in this book began to feel once they started the process of finding the facts, and abandoning guesswork. Nearly every story in this book reflects companies that have guessed wrong about what's of value to their customers. The stories in this chapter show you how getting it right has paid dividends.

Entegra Roof Tile has been manufacturing concrete roof tile in South Florida since 1986. A highly environmentally conscious company, Entegra is a member of the

Tile Roofing Institute, and is committed to conserving our environmental resources. Entegra's beautiful tiles are made from natural materials including sand, cement, clay, and water-based sealers. Natural pigments are added for coloring. Entegra's tiles provide the highest fire protection available, and are designed to be strong and durable. That longevity keeps them from adding to the tremendous volume of other roofing materials that burden landfills. In fact, Entegra roof tiles often outlast the structures they span.

Owners (and brothers) Terry and Mike Johnson were pretty sure that they knew what their customers, roofing contractors, wanted most. They thought that their customers' top priority was *the ability to buy directly* from Entegra, the manufacturer, and avoid middlemen. And they believed the *outstanding quality* of Entegra tiles came next.

The brothers' assessment was half right. The contractors valued *the outstanding quality of their tiles,* but ranked *ability to buy directly from Entegra* tenth on the list. The other two top attributes were *predictable delivery times*, and *quick response to complaints.*

The brothers immediately focused on what the roofing contractors said they wanted most. They posted the top three survey results on the company website. Next to each one they posted statistics that documented Entegra's excellence in providing what customers really want. Finally, they included a statement that I consider the epitome of relevant selling because it clearly tells customers that Entegra delivers what they want most. Here's how it reads:

ENTEGRA ROOF TILE IS THE SOUTH FLORIDA MANUFACTURERS ASSOCIATION'S "MANUFACTURER OF THE YEAR."

In addition, Entegra received the highest rating of any tile manufacturer for offering the "Overall Best Value for the Price" in a blind marketing survey. This survey of Florida roofing contractors revealed their top three priorities in selecting a roof tile manufacturer. The results indicate they want:

TOP 3 PRIORITIES	HOW ENTEGRA DELIVERED
Tile that is consistent in weight, size, density, strength and color. ➡	Based on 2010 data, less than 2 orders per 1,000 resulted in a complaint regarding manufacturing quality from our Okeechobee facility.
A company that will resolve issues quickly. ➡	Of the issues we did experience in 2010, 92% were acknowledged within one business day, 82% were resolved within one week and 86% were completely resolved within 2 weeks.

Reliable and predictable service.	➡	In 2010, 98% of the orders delivered by Entegra were shipped in f\ull on the scheduled date communicated to our customers. An additional 1% of the orders, which could not be delivered on a single truck, were shipped in full by the end of the next business day.

After a major hurricane hit South Florida several years ago, Entegra was inundated with orders. As they poured in, Terry and Mike realized that the demand for roofing tiles was more than they would be able to supply. "We took the orders that we could fill and turned down those we knew we couldn't deliver," Mike said. "Although some of our customers were upset, we didn't string them along; we set them free to look elsewhere. We felt that it was more important for customers to know the truth up front than to learn later that we couldn't deliver."

Entegra's decision paid off. It showed that the company had integrity and didn't promise what they couldn't provide. Entegra's integrity made their sales messages more believable and kept intact the company's reputation for making prompt deliveries. By refusing business that they couldn't fill, Mike and Terry built confidence and removed risk from their customers' buying decisions. By focusing on and communicating that which is most important, in a positively horrible construction market, they have gained hard fought for market share.

Continually remind your customers how well you have performed. Frequent reminders are necessary because when customers get what they want they may take it for granted. Many of our clients are successful because they are superb at solving problems. But they're *not* good at *saying so*. If this applies to you, you're short-changing yourself and your company. And maybe your sales!

RESISTANCE AND DENIAL

Like individuals, companies have blind spots. They can be arrogant, myopic, and in denial. The passion that drives many business leaders to succeed can be a double-edged sword. One side can furnish the force that drives them to succeed, but the other can blind them and prevent them from recognizing what others clearly see.

"Too many executives claim to know what customers want better than the customers themselves," according to Seena Sharp of Sharp Market Intelligence (a competitive intelligence firm). "And when the executive is wrong about his/her view of the customer, the customer is viewed as the problem and as being disloyal. The reality is that the company has abandoned the customer by not improving or addressing customer concerns. Customers prefer to stay with the product or service they know and, once a customer, they will give you considerable leeway before defecting."

Seena is right. Incredibly, when my consulting team shows survey results to companies and they learn that their customers' top buying criteria are not what they think, they sometimes refuse to accept it. Some are simply in denial while others insist that the survey results are wrong. They come up with all sorts of arguments: the survey was not conducted correctly; the sampling was not reflective; the respondents' value systems were flawed; the finding might be valid for other companies, but not for them. One client quit our process midstream because they refused to accept the customer feedback.

Frequently, businesses are started because the founders see a particular niche that needs to be filled and they come up with a good way to fill it. Usually, the founders have extensive in-depth knowledge, and experience in their field. They're experts who have been successful, know all the players, and know how everything works. So when they receive survey results that are not consistent with their beliefs or run counter to their instincts, they may be unable to accept them. They may contend that the results are wrong, and that they have a better overall understanding of the business and their customers' needs than those surveyed.

Some decision makers may be unable to accept customer survey results because they have not kept up with the times. For years, they enjoyed relative calm and their businesses ran smoothly and profitably. Then the business environment changed and fast-paced evolution became the rule. Upstarts penetrated many markets, and companies that didn't change often got stampeded. The traditional print book publishing industry is a prime example. Self-publishing and ebooks are taking buckets of market share from them every day.

So, many leaders were overwhelmed or could not fully grasp new technology, or industry and economic developments, and their far-reaching implications. Some were slow to see that their businesses, methods, or procedures had become outdated and obsolete. Eastman Kodak immediately comes to mind.

MAJOR COMPANIES

You might think this is a problem just for small businesses, but it affects all companies: large, medium, and small. To illustrate the importance of asking crucial questions of customers, I'd like to give you a few examples from some giant international companies.

Biogel is a leading surgical brand of Mölnlycke Health Care, a Swedish medical devices giant. Founded in 1849, Mölnlycke manufactures single-use surgical and wound care products and services for health care professionals. Biogel sells hundreds of millions pairs of surgical gloves to hospitals and doctors in every corner of the globe.

When we began this assignment, Biogel had the

premier product, but tough competition had taken thirty-five percent of their market share in the U.K. The company was losing share in a number of markets. The problem was that Biogel's gloves carried an average forty percent price premium. To compound the problem, the U.K.'s National Health Service pressured procurement managers to buy on price.

Biogel's salespeople had lost confidence. They didn't know how to overcome their product's price disadvantage. Some were at a loss, paralyzed, and close to surrender.

At the request of their global team, we went to Manchester, England, and took Biogel's executive management team through our Smart Advantage Process. In it, we identified over sixty-five potential competitive advantages that Biogel was either not using, or not using well, in their marketing messages. Just knowing they had such a list of advantages made everyone at Biogel very excited, but we cautioned them to hold their horses.

When you approach customers, don't overwhelm them or take a scattergun approach. If you reel off sixty-seven reasons why they should buy from you, your most relevant competitive advantages are likely to be buried and lost in the boredom. For example, at a workshop in Washington D.C. a few years ago, the vice president of sales for a $13-billion pump manufacturer headquartered in Dublin, Ireland, told me her salespeople had a tendency to "show up and throw up." This is not a good sales tactic.

Instead, learn what is most important to each of your customers before you make your pitch. Find out what deliverables your customer wants most from you; the top reasons why he or she will buy from you. Then list your competitive advantages in the order your customer ranked them.

My left-brained partner likes to talk about his 80-20 *squared* rule for sales. Most salespeople know to spend eighty percent of their face time listening and only twenty percent talking. To square it, spend eighty percent of your talking time *asking questions*, and the remaining twenty percent of your talking time actually *proving* to your customer how well you have delivered exactly what they want (which you now know because you asked formally through research, and you listened).

The Biogel team asked us to find what each of their three levels of customer for their surgical gloves valued. The three were hospital procurement managers, operating room managers, and surgeons. The research survey revealed that surgeons wanted gloves with a history of very few complaints.

Fortunately, Biogel had strong metrics that their salespeople could emphasize. They could tell customers, "We receive the fewest complaints of any glove producer. We average less than 2.8 complaints per million gloves sold." Before we identified Biogel's competitive advantages, their salespeople rarely touted the fact that the company received so few complaints. (By the way, Six Sigma is 3.4

defects per million parts. Biogel's complaint rate is better than that. Wouldn't *you* brag about it?)

We also found that glove quality was literally of life or death importance. A hole in a glove during surgery could expose operating room staff to HIV, hepatitis, and a host of other blood-borne diseases. Again, Biogel had the metrics. The company's gloves had the lowest number of holes in the industry. Their Acceptable Quality Level (AQL, a standard industry measure) for holes was thirty-five percent better than their closest competitor. Why? Because every single glove is air inflated specifically to test for holes at the factory.

Besides being far less likely to have a hole in the first place, punctures or tears in Biogel gloves could be detected more quickly than those in competitors' products. Only Biogel's gloves had a patented technology that enabled people to detect a puncture within seconds. Spotting holes in competitors' gloves took much longer, creating greater risk of contamination.

CUSTOMIZING SALES TOOLS

After gathering the measurements on the highest-rated attributes, we met with Biogel's U. K. sales team. We handed out a list of the top four attributes that each target market said most influenced their buying decisions. We followed that by showing them how respondents rated Biogel on the highest rated attributes, compared with their three top competitors. The results were clear: those surveyed preferred Biogel over their competitors. Finally we handed out a sales tool we had designed that incorporated these facts and data proving Biogel's competitive advantage statements, relevant to each of the top attributes, and compared to their top two competitors. When the salespeople received these tools, the room grew deathly silent.

The silence threw me; I was really concerned. Did I make some grave mistake or cultural faux pas? After all, we were in Penang, Malaysia, after thirty hours flying, suffering a twelve-hour time shift, and speaking American with the Brits. Finally, I summoned the courage to ask, "Could I please have some feedback?"

Still silence. Absolute silence. Finally, after a few moments, a woman simply said, "Brilliant!" I didn't know then that "brilliant" was British for "marvelous," and frankly I was expecting pushback on the price premium.

I openly chuckled and asked for more feedback. Another person said, "Fantastic!" Almost immediately, everyone began speaking at once. They were ecstatic and told us, "This gives us lots of ammunition and makes us more confident about our glove's advantages."

Then I asked, "Do you think this information will enable you to overcome your product's price premium?"

And I loved the reply: "Absolutely!"

The sales force returned to Manchester, *united* (sorry, I just couldn't resist!) as a team. The next year, Biogel

U.K. exceeded their sales quotas. As of the last reports, the company is still winning the battle against their competitors for market share despite very tough market conditions.

DANGEROUS ASSUMPTION

Impetuous and overconfident business leaders ask for trouble when they change their strategies without learning and factoring in what their customers prize. Even the biggest and brightest guess and may not look before they leap. Even Mark Zuckerberg, the founding genius of Facebook, the spectacularly successful online social network, fell into this trap.

Thanks to the award-winning hit movie *The Social Network*, Zuckerberg's story is well known. As a Harvard undergrad, he and some classmates started Facebook, and he built the company according to what he instinctively thought students wanted. Founded in 2004, Facebook's ascent has been meteoric: according to *Business Insider*, by the end of 2011 they had more than 845 million active users worldwide and revenue of over $3.7 billion. They claim to have taken in a net income of nearly $1 billion in 2011. The Facebook mobile app is the most down-loaded app on all smart phones; by December 2011 they had more than 425 million mobile users.

Since Zuckerberg's gut feelings were so spot-on when he started and built Facebook, it stands to reason that he would continue to make assumptions in running the social network. He added a feature to Facebook called News Feed, which automatically communicated members' activities to all their Facebook friends. News Feed created an uproar. Members hated News Feed because it could invade their privacy and disclose information about their sensitive personal relationships. For example, it could spread the word that members were romantically involved even though they wanted to keep the nature of their relationships secret.

Soon after News Feed launched, Facebook was inundated with more than 700,000 online petitions from irate members. Many were furious that their personal secrets were publicly aired. They demanded that Facebook pull the plug on the social network's all-too-revealing new feature.

Eventually, Zuckerberg backed off. According to an account in *Information Week*, he admitted that he had really messed up. News Feed was redesigned to give members privacy protection. Now, they have the option to control who can see their postings.

Facebook could have easily and inexpensively avoided this mistake. Before News Feed was rolled out, the company could have polled members and sought their feedback. Instead of getting a black eye, Zuckerberg and Facebook could have strengthened their relationship with their members and built goodwill by consulting them before the launch. They would have found out what their members wanted, or didn't want, and given them a voice in Facebook's decision-making process.

Mark Zuckerberg clearly learned his lesson. In a January 14, 2012 *Wall Street Journal* interview he stated, "People used to say to me that in order for Facebook to work, we somehow needed to sell out. The best way for Facebook to work is to do exactly what people want."

CHANGING DESIRES

Many of us grew up loving Wonder Bread because of advertisements that convinced us that it "Helps Build Strong Bodies 8 Ways" (subsequently increased to 12 ways). Sadly, that storied brand did not keep up with changing times. According to Seena Sharp, when those in charge decided to turn the Wonder Bread company into toast in 2004, they said, "The company was in the wrong business in the wrong market."

So it came as a big surprise when, a week after Wonder Bread crumbled, rival baker Pepperidge Farm announced that they were about to launch three new whole-grain white breads. "Consumers love the taste of white bread, but are looking for healthier, more nutritious options," Pepperidge Farm declared.

"How can one company see defeat where another sees opportunity?" Sharp asked. "Wonder Bread *blames* the customer for shrinking sales, while Pepperidge Farm *courts* the customer by giving them what they want: the comfort of white bread with the health benefits of whole grains."

Follow Pepperidge Farm's lead. Ask your customers and listen to them. Since their needs and desires change, make soliciting information from your customers a continuous part of your business. If you constantly look for changes, you can move quickly when they occur and stay relevant by delivering what your customers want. Like yesterday's lovers of not-so-nutritious white bread, your customers may now crave a healthier diet.

COFFEE, TEA, OR SORBETTO

Since 1971, Starbucks has grown from a single cafe in Seattle, Washington to more than 17,000 outlets in more than fifty-five countries. They serve millions of discerning customers every day.

But even the most successful companies have lapses. Starbucks was hit hard by the recession and forced to close some nine hundred locations. To boost company sales in 2008, CEO Howard Schultz introduced a new drink, Sorbetto. The ingredients for Sorbetto were imported from Italy, and with great fanfare the new drink was introduced at three hundred Starbucks locations in the United States.

Sorbetto bombed, big time. Customers found it too sweet, and Starbucks' baristas, who could have pushed to boost its sales, despised the drink because after a hard day on their feet they had to spend an hour and a half cleaning the special Sorbetto machines. When Starbucks discontinued Sorbetto, Schultz admitted that in introducing Sorbetto, he impulsively moved too fast.

Starbucks learned an important lesson. When they introduced Via, their instant coffee brand, the company didn't make the same mistake. Since 2006, Starbucks had been developing Via, and before it hit the street, they conducted customer research. Instead of having a big Sorbetto-like rollout, Starbucks had blind tastings in two cities and conducted focus groups. When the research yielded positive results, Starbucks took Via nationwide. In 2010, Via sales exceeded $200 million and is being sold internationally and in retail outlets.

Starbucks has become more customer conscious. In another move to lure back customers, Starbucks is making their locations more customer-friendly. Cookie-cutter store designs are out; new shops have a warmer and friendlier feel. They also fit in with and reflect their neighborhoods better. Starbucks has expanded their coffee offerings by selling some rare coffees, the kind previously offered only by specialty roasters.

Despite the company's size, power, and market dominance, Starbucks still works at being relevant. They learn what their customers want by keeping their fingers on their caffeinated pulses.

On the company's website, www.starbucks.com, their *My Starbucks Idea* solicits customer feedback and discussion on that feedback. Here's what it says:

"You know better than anyone else what you want from Starbucks. So tell us. What's your Starbucks Idea? Revolutionary or simple – we want to hear it. Share your ideas, tell us what you think of other people's ideas and join the discussion. We're here, and we're ready to make ideas happen. Let's get started."

Not only does Starbucks solicit their customers' suggestions, they implement them. Then they capitalize on those facts in their new ads (this from a company famous for not advertising). In the process, Starbucks portrays themselves as customer centric, a good listener, and an upstanding company that graciously thanks their customers and gives them credit. In a nutshell, the company wins all around by getting new product ideas, building good will, and appearing to be grateful to their customers.

Since every company now has a website, think about using yours to reach out to your customers and get their views.

MEDIA EXPERTS

Even some of the top experts guess rather than ask. Take 352 Media Group, a highly successful company that designs award-winning websites and interactive media campaigns, and is recognized for their invention and creativity. This Gainesville, Florida company has developed more than a thousand websites, web applications, phone apps, and interactive marketing campaigns for businesses and organizations around the globe.

The 352 story embodies the American dream. The company that ultimately became 352 started as a part-time student venture to help three students pay their way through school. At the University of Florida, Geoff Wilson (the current 352 CEO), along with Jesse Murse and Brian Keller started designing web pages from a room in their fraternity house. Within two years, their startup had thirty active clients and the workload became too demanding to handle along with a full college course load.

So Geoff scaled back his studies to focus full-time on business.

By 2009, 352 had over sixty employees and had received numerous awards. For the third year in a row it was ranked on *Inc.* magazine's list of the 5,000 fastest-growing privately held companies in America, and was selected as one of the Top 100 fastest-growing Marketing Service Agencies in the United States by *AdAge* Magazine. *BtoB* Magazine named it one of the top interactive agencies in the United States, and it was selected as one of the nation's Top Three Web Design Companies by TopSEOs. com. 352 Media Group has won more than one hundred ADDY® Awards, including several awards in distinct competitions.

You get the idea. If any company should know what a website should convey, it would be 352. But they too went astray. The company's website wasn't relevant because it didn't deliver messages that said what 352's prospects and customers wanted to hear.

The centerpiece of their website was a clever, entertaining, and beautifully produced video hosted by Geoff Wilson and his marketing chief Peter VanRysdam. The video took a light-hearted approach, and was packed with humor and colorful, eye-catching graphics that stressed 352's strengths. The video and their website gave prospects an example of the outstanding work 352 turned out.

In the video, the first three items that 352 touted were (1) *the awards* the company had won for web design, (2) their numerous *Fortune 500 and well-known clients* and (3) the fact that they had *more than fifty people on their team.*

We tested these three attributes in a survey 352 commissioned to learn what prospects and customers wanted most from a web design firm. The respondents were asked to rank twenty-one attributes in order of importance. Those surveyed reported that the top three items plugged in 352's video were the least important to them. *Design awards* came in at number nineteen, *Fortune 500 clients* at twenty, and *number of employees* dead last.

Even the sharpest and savviest businesses can wander off course and deliver irrelevant sales messages. When 352 got the survey results, Geoff Wilson realized, "Our core messages were the least important things to our market. People love our video, compliment me on it all the time and tell me how great is – but no one has ever told me that the message is effective."

Let's look at the top five items that those surveyed said they wanted most from a web design firm. Item #1 was *the ability to respond quickly,* which 352 knew at the time was not one of their core strengths. Since then, the company has made quick response to clients' requests a top priority. Second was *ability to assess clients' needs and incorporate them,* third was *the granting of full ownership of final product and source code to clients,* fourth came *adherence to schedule,* and fifth was *knowing all costs up front.* All were strengths of 352's but 352 wasn't touting them in any of its marketing messages (check out their website now at www.352media.com). This knowledge has accelerated the growth of an already successful company.

Watch out for this trap! You may be considered an expert; you know your specialty, field, or industry inside out. You may be paid top dollar to provide your expertise. However, the true experts are your prospects and customers because only they know what they want. To be an expert, don't guess why your prospects and customers buy. Find out.

Remember the pest control company in Chapter One? They were about to gamble a quarter-million dollars on an advertising message that they *guessed* their target market valued most. For a little more than a fifth of that, they commissioned a double-blind survey that told them they were wrong, and saved them from wasting a big chunk of their advertising budget.

REPLACE GUESSWORK WITH RELEVANCE

- What messages do you push most in your advertising and sales pitches? How do you *know* that they are relevant to your target market?
- Check your assumptions. What do you *assume* is a given in your industry or sector?
- Do you think you know what your customers want, better than your customers do? Have any customers defected? Were you able to learn if it was because you were not being relevant?
- Perhaps you actually have what your customers want. But since you don't *know* how important it might be to them, you haven't articulated how good you are, and your claims sound more like promises. What "promises" exist in your marketing materials? In your sales pitches?
- What current, formal effort do you have in place to find out what your customers really want, *à la* Starbucks?
- When was the last time you adjusted your marketing and sales messaging to ensure it was relevant to today's concerns and today's buyers? Too often companies use the same message year after year after year. This may work for a slogan or jingle – "It's the real thing" or "Plop, plop, fizz, fizz" – but even these are dated. It may be time for you to test for relevance.

CHAPTER 4

Relevant Selling Relies on Internal Agreement
Very Few Companies Have It

YOUR FAVORITE TEAM HAS THE FOOTBALL. THE offensive unit breaks from the huddle, runs crisply to the scrimmage line, and everyone moves into position for the play. The quarterback barks the signals, the ball is snapped, and everyone moves forward – except for two players. They go off on their own in completely different directions, and are out of synch with the rest of the team. So the play breaks down and the team doesn't advance. In fact, it's thrown for a loss.

How long do you think a professional team that played like that would last? Ask the infamous 1976

Tampa Bay Buccaneers, who won *none* of their fourteen games and were named the worst team in NFL history. "The coach (John McKay) stopped talking to us after the third game," defensive lineman Pat Toomay told the *Columbus Dispatch* in 2001. "During the week, he wanted nothing to do with us. I can't blame him, really."

Your company may not be losing all its games, but consider the following quote from Richard A. D'Aveni, professor of strategic management at Dartmouth's College's Tuck School of Business.

"Whenever I've asked senior executives to map the positions of their company's brands and those of key rivals, we end up confused and dismayed," wrote D'Aveni in the *Harvard Business Review* (September 20, 2008). "Different executives place their firm's offerings in different spots on a price benefit map, few know the primary benefit their products offer, and they all overestimate the benefits of their own offerings while underestimating those of their rivals."

Our statistics show that ninety-eight percent of the time, significant differences exist in-house on what customers want most. The head of one department thinks customers want something different from what the head of another department believes. When these key figures are not on the same page, and they act according to their individual beliefs, the company's resources can be more scattered than the contents of a teenager's bedroom. The company's focus can be diluted and its profits can fall short. When internal perceptions vary, resources, energy, and accountability tend to be diluted and wasted; companies are less likely to operate efficiently and more likely to fall short of their goals.

Discordant perceptions cause confusion. When key people pursue diverse goals, your employees don't know who to listen to or what to do. Differing personal beliefs within your company can prevent you from delivering consistent relevant messages.

These varying perceptions among key people exist regardless of the company's products, or services, or size. The problem occurs because leaders don't actually know what their customers' top priorities are – so they guess.

WORKING THE PROCESS

When we work with a company, as one step in designing our market research questionnaire we compile a list of attributes that are based on a company team brainstorming session, and which is designed to uncover potential competitive advantages and disadvantages. Then we whittle down the list to those the team *thinks* their customers value most in their buying decisions (after all, a company can't be *completely* wrong and stay in business long). And we whittle the list some more to get down to the maximum number we know we can test in a telephone interview.

The research is conducted and the findings tabulated. As previously described, we then ask the management team to vote on how they think their prospects and customers ranked those attributes. Specifically, we ask them to rank the attributes that they think buyers rated first, second, third, and last. We ask team members to include their title with their votes. Then we compare the aggregate of their votes to the actual market research results. We also look closely at the votes from different departments or functions within each company.

As I described briefly in Chapter One, a typical result looks like this: the head of production believes that the quality of the company's product is customers' number one criterion, while the chief of sales insists that customers buy on the basis of price and their relationships with salespeople. Or the head of HR is convinced, not surprisingly, that the level of expertise of the company's personnel is their differentiator.

When decision makers are not in agreement, each will work to deliver what he or she thinks customers most prefer. We all know that when everyone in a company is not singing from the same hymnal, it can weaken the company's strategic focus, resulting in irrelevant customer messages. It can prevent companies from serving their customers well. So why do companies let these disparate views prevail?

The answer is simple. Most companies don't know that differing views exist! Usually, they don't find out about the differences until we ask their people to rank the list of tested attributes. When we get their answers, the internal differences are clear. Lack of internal consensus means lack of external consensus on who you are and what you stand for. Remember the old sales adage – if you confuse 'em, you lose 'em. And that's especially true if your answers are not relevant to your market.

If you're masochistic enough to play golf, you know all too well the importance of hitting the ball dead center. If you don't strike it just right, even if you just marginally miss the sweet spot, you could end up trudging through the trees or digging your ball out of the sand (I do that a lot!). Ultimately, you'll probably get to the hole, but it will take longer, won't be much fun, and your score will drop.

In business, it's costly to squander your time and resources, take extra strokes, and wander off course. All your team members should know your customers' sweet spots and constantly focus on them. We've seen our clients gain that focus by learning exactly what their customers want most. When they do, they hit that sweet spot, close more sales, and gain market share without having to cave in on price.

AGREEING ON A PATH

In Chapter Two I told you about Armellini Express Lines, Inc., the highly service-oriented floral transport company. When we began to work with Armellini, they initially had some internal disagreements over what their customers wanted most. Some were certain that a lower price was the key to success, while others cited other attributes.

"Before we went through the Smart Advantage process, all of our people were not on the same page," said company CEO David Armellini. "They didn't all agree on what our customers wanted most and what our competitive advantages were. Their beliefs depended on their position. For example, our salespeople had different ideas and, therefore, they pushed different things. Often, it depended on the length of their tenure with us and their relationships with their customers. So we next surveyed our customers to find out what *they* wanted."

We ask every client this question for starters: What do you think your company's number one competitive advantage is? Generally, if we have fifteen people in the room we get fifteen different answers. On our first visit, Armellini's staff came up with this list:

- Experience
- Service
- Resources
- Trust
- Quality
- One-stop shop
- Online services
- Reliable
- Price
- Billing

Sound like your company? This is very typical of a first cut at this question. The clichés come up every time. On our second visit with the executive team, before we revealed the research results, we showed them the list of tested attributes and asked them to select the three they thought their customers valued most.

Key members of Armellini's executive team thought that their customers' top priority was *on-time deliveries*. David Armellini, his vice president of sales and marketing, and his vice president of driver operations all ranked *on-time deliveries* as number one. Two salespeople who placed *on-time deliveries* second in importance to customers, were also in the target zone.

One of their sales reps and a customer service executive each thought that *ease of operations* – having few forms and rules – was most important. However, five other executives each placed some other attribute first. This divergence of opinion is not only common, it borders on being universal. In our study of more than one hundred companies, we found the same data scatter for virtually every company when voting on what they thought their prospects and customers preferred.

If Armellini's president and his V.P. of sales & marketing believed that customers wanted *on-time deliveries*, but other key executives disagreed, how could Armellini send a consistent message to their customers? And without internal agreement, how can the company operationally ensure that they deliver what is most demanded?

"After we got the survey results," David Armellini said, "we brought in all our salespeople. Different sales-people had been telling different customers different things, so we stressed the importance of communicating consistently, saying the same relevant things. We went over our competitive advantages with our sales force, made sure they understood them, and showed them how to sell them. We created a brochure that bullet-pointed our relevant competitive advantages and explained how we wanted our salespeople to explain them to our customers. Our sales force offered no resistance because they realized that we were giving them an asset – infor-mation that would boost their sales.

"This process gave us a unified message to deliver to customers. Prior to going through the process, we touched our customers in different ways. After the process, we put together a consistent pitch to present to customers. Instead of one salesperson selling it this way and another taking a different approach, we now had a consistent voice. That consistent voice extended beyond our salespeople. We used it in customer service, at conferences, and at conventions."

WINE MAKING KITS

Even the most successful and profitable companies can have significant differences in their internal percep-tions of customers' values. When they do, these varying perceptions can keep companies from reaching their full potential.

Home wine making is big business in Canada, and growing elsewhere. More than 1,400 retail stores sell wine kits for home vintners in Canada alone. A manufacturer of home winemaking kits brought us in to help improve their marketing message and sales efforts.

We worked with seventeen staff members, and asked each to list what he or she thought were customers' top three preferences. We requested them to rank their guesses first, second, and third, in accordance with how important they thought each item was to the company's customers.

The differences were typical.

- No two salespeople agreed on what customers valued most.
- The president and the marketing manager both chose the *manufacturer's investment in marketing and advertising for the retailer* as their top choice, while only three other employees ranked that attribute anywhere in the top three.
- As his second choice, the president selected *the level of support by sales reps*, but only three other employees ranked that attribute in the top three.
- Six employees ranked *on-time delivery* highly. Neither the president nor the director of marketing included it on their lists.
- Each of the account managers responded differently.

One chose *quality/reputation of the lab or processing facility* as most important, another picked *order fill rate* as the highest, while the third placed *money-back guarantee* atop his list.

If you're grimacing about now, you probably should be. I dare you to try this exercise with your team!

Opposite (Figure 4-A) is a partial list of the attributes tested, so you can see for yourself how the votes of the wine kit manufacturer were scattered.

An interesting follow-up: the market research showed that one of the top three attributes was *freshness of wine kits*. The company was chagrined when they received important feedback from a new hire during our second company visit. She relayed that during her orientation, the warehouse staff told her that the question most frequently asked by customers when they toured the company's facility was, "How do we know that we are buying your freshest wine kits?" The manufacturer's management was stunned. They had no idea how important the *freshness of the wine kits* was to the company's customers.

Since they already had good metrics for the other top attributes, the manufacturer was now able to address freshness by describing the variety of locations of their vineyards, the criteria the company uses to choose vineyards, the frequency at which they make juice, the benefit of the date stamping on the kits, etc.

FIGURE 4-A

VOTES - HIERARCHY OF BUYING CRITERIA

ATTRIBUTES	Most Important			Least
	#1	#2	#3	
Quality/reputation of the manufacturer's lab or processing facility	3	1		
On-time delivery	6			
Transparency in freight costs				1
Freshness of wine kits			1	
Money-back guarantee on product	1		1	
Availability of electronic order entry				2
Level of technical support available to the retailer		1		1
Level of technical support available to the consumer				1
Manufacturer's investment in marketing and advertising for the retailer	2	1	2	
Level of support by sales representative	1	1	2	
Order accuracy (how accurately your order was filled)	1	3	3	
Order fill rate (did you receive 100% of what you ordered)	2	4	1	

Internal disagreements are not an indictment of this manufacturer; nearly every company we studied has had similar internal disconnects. Applause for the manufacturer for taking the time and making the effort to align their staff and their sales and marketing messages with their customers' most crucial concerns.

AGREEING ON THE WRONG THING

There is another common, and potentially dangerous, disparity between a company's view and their customers' view. Sometimes we get significant internal consistency on what managers think their customers value most when making a buying decision, but that internal agreement doesn't match reality.

More than half of a steel fabricator's executives thought that their number one competitive advantage – the value they offered that differentiated them from their competitors – was the breadth and depth of their inventory. This attribute ranked *eighth* on the double-blind survey. Not one person on the executive team guessed the attribute most important to their customers – *accuracy and completeness of documentation*. "We thought that was a given."

In Chapter One, I introduced you to Big Five Tours & Expeditions, the high-end tour wholesaler. In its early years, Big Five specialized in African safaris, so the company name pays homage to the five animals big game hunters find most difficult to hunt on foot: lions, cape buffaloes, elephants, black rhinos, and panthers (not to worry – Big Five does only photographic safaris). Big

Fives travel products are the "experience of a lifetime" trips we all dream about.

When we polled Big Five's staff to discover what they thought their customers valued most, the answers were also widely diverse.

- One employee thought *responsiveness to complaints* was most important.
- Two declared *level of tour experience of staff* was the top attribute.
- Two placed *speed of commission payment* as number one.
- One employee was sure that *clarity of pricing* should top the list.
- One ranked *availability of hotline for emergency support* first.

In fact, of the twenty attributes we tested, thirteen of them received votes in the top three. This type of data spread occurs when your staff doesn't really know what your customers value.

On the other hand, seven of Big Five's staff members agreed that *turnaround time on proposals* was one of the most important attributes. "Wow," we thought, "we have some agreement here." The problem was, the consensus was on the wrong deliverable, not on what Big Five's customers valued most. They were in agreement about the wrong thing. Oops! In fact, travel agents didn't even rate *turnaround time on proposals* in the top ten items they looked for when choosing a tour operator. So here a group of employees was working hard to provide fast turnaround time, when it wasn't nearly as highly valued as they always thought it to be.

WIDE DATA SCATTER

A company that provides financial education and asset management offered a relatively expensive investment education course. They wanted to find out what factors drove people to attend their course. Going in, they believed that their prime target markets were people who were familiar with their company and the course they offered, followed by people who wanted to do some investing on their own.

We asked the leadership team to identify the three attributes they thought their customers and prospective customers valued most and the one they felt was least important. The data scatter was as wide as any we've seen. Here's the spread:

- Six voted for *availability of tools to manage investments independently.*
- Eight execs voted for *referrals from people you know* (but one considered that the least important attribute).
- Two said *ease of access to staff.*
- Two answered *ongoing support after the course.*
- Two voted for *clarity of pricing.* (One employee voted

for this attribute as least important, when in fact, it was their collective customers' top priority.)

Unfortunately, the attributes that the leadership agreed upon, such as *referrals from people you know* and *availability of tools to manage investments independently*, were not ranked highly by the company's customers. Again, there was agreement, but it was about the wrong thing. In fact, customers ranked *referrals from people you know* ninth. This indicates that when people think about learning how to make financial investments, they don't rely on testimonials or endorsements; they make their own decisions. *Availability of tools to manage investments independently* came in fifth with customers.

For most companies, the big "Aha!" moment comes when they compare the data scatter with the attributes that their customers ranked highest. And diligent teams make sure that their decision making and messaging are internally and externally aligned with their customers' perceptions.

PEST CONTROL COMPANY

Established in 1951, Nozzle Nolen is a South Florida-based pest control company that serves more than twenty thousand monthly customers in an area known for its profusion of glamorous, ultra-luxurious homes and estates. Prestigious Jupiter Island is among their client-list ZIP codes. The recipient of the Better Business Bureau's Golden Bee Award, Nozzle Nolen is the first pest control company in Florida to offer Green Shield Certified services from the IPM Institute of North America. Each year, Nozzle Nolen averages over five thousand hours of training, and is the only pest control company to offer treatment service "on time or on us."

Talk about scattered and divergent opinions – look at this spread. Of the twenty attributes we tested with management, six received first place votes. And on the other end of the spectrum, eleven of the twenty attributes got votes for last place. Since Nozzle Nolen sells directly to consumers, leadership thought that the main reasons customers hired them was because of the *recommendation of a relative or friend*, but they were wrong. The customer market research found that the number one buying criteria for prospects and customers was *billing accuracy*, which only three of the twenty leaders polled placed in their top three, and no one voted it first.

Figure 4-B shows how Nozzle Nolen's management differed in what they thought were their customers' hierarchy of buying criteria. Again, please note that this scatter is representative of the more than a hundred companies in our study. Odds are good you will find it in your company too.

FIGURE 4-B

ATTRIBUTES	Most Important			Least
	#1	#2	#3	
Financial stability of company				3
All employees pass strict screening and background checks	1	1	2	
Widely recognized company	3	1	3	
Speed of response to service request	4	3	1	
Number of homes serviced in our community				1
Recommendation of neighbor or friend	9	3	1	
Length of guarantee on service				2
Service awards from business groups (BBB, Angie's List, etc.)		2	1	1
Knowledge of sales reps		4	1	
Use of pet-friendly products		1	1	
Money back guarantee if not on time				2
Company services local hospitals, zoos, etc.				3
High percentage of referral business	1		1	1
Courteous sales and service technicians			3	
Online billing/bill payment options			1	2
Ability to handle all pests: insects, mammals, reptiles, weeds				1
Billing accuracy		1	2	
Ease of scheduling appointment with company		2	2	
Locally owned business		1	1	2
Quick response to new invasive insects, e.g., citrus aphids, fig white fly	2	1		2

Let me give you further details on management's differences. Only the company president, Mickey Nolen, listed the top three attributes in the same order as the majority of the management team. The item he named as least important also agreed with management's vote; however, after that, the differences were great. The general manager thought that customers wanted *speed of response to service request* most, followed by *all employees pass strict screening and background checks,* and *billing accuracy.* The secretary/treasurer, who handles accounts payable, guessed that customers' top priority was *all employees pass strict screening and background checks*, that *widely recognized company* was second, and *online billing/bill payment options* third. A branch manager listed *recommendation or friend of neighbor* first, *knowledge of sales reps* second, and *use of pet-friendly products* third. Another branch manager agreed that *recommendation of a neighbor or friend* should be first, but thought *locally owned business* came next followed by *courteous sales and service technicians.*

Once again, I want to emphasize that the examples presented are not exceptions. I'm sorry to say, they're the rule. So be on the lookout. Most people don't look for internal disagreements, and they can be hard to spot. They can derail the best of efforts to grow. And remember, you can't fix what you don't know is broken.

ALIGNING PERCEPTIONS

When we see signs of internal dissonance about perceptions of customers' values, we make sure our clients understand why these discrepancies can cause problems. So we ask department heads some basic questions that usually drive our points home.

- Ask your teammates, staff, and/or executive team these questions: What do you think are the top three things that customers value most when choosing to buy your product/service? What do you think is the least important? Collect the responses and record the answers.
- Make a note of the data scatter that is likely to result. When you do this exercise, ask the team to put their titles on their votes. See if you can find consistent themes based on their job functions.
- Notice if different disciplines in your organization are in agreement. Awareness is the first step toward any improvement.
- What are your management objectives based on? Have you ensured that they are most relevant to your customers?
- Is management investing and applying resources according to their unaligned views? Try Professor D'Aveni's brand mapping exercise, described at the beginning of the chapter. See what your sales team or your executive team thinks of your brand, your competitors' brands, and their comparative value (price benefit, in his words).

- Review a sample of your marketing material. What are the three most prominent messages? How do you know they are relevant?
- What are the three most consistent themes in your sales messages? Do they match what you found in the marketing materials? Are *they* relevant?

It is probably not a big surprise that a company's ignorance of its customers' values sometimes results in a lack of good internal communication. Let your customer feedback – not how good you are, but what's important to them – serve as your company GPS. This data can efficiently guide you to your ultimate goal. Basing internal communication and decisions on solid customer data rather than on a host of guesses, or a lot of left turns, is a much smarter strategy.

CHAPTER 5

Prospects and Customers Have Different Hot Buttons

Relevant Selling Means Knowing How They Differ

W HEN WE ANALYZED THE RESEARCH FINDINGS for the companies in our study, we frequently observed differences between the buying criteria of those companies' prospects and the buying criteria of their existing customers. We saw, in company after company, a pattern that was not an anomaly, but rather a trend. In about seventy percent of the surveys, what prospects said they wanted when choosing a company was statistically different from what existing customers said they wanted.

Then, when we looked at the sales messaging that

companies used for both their prospects and for their customer retention pitches, we noticed little or no difference. That meant that one of the messages was pretty much guaranteed to be irrelevant.

Over the years, we have worked with all kinds of companies ranging from the tiniest start-ups to the largest global organizations. In the process, we defined what we consider prospect and customer variations. While some sales professionals consider all sales targets homogeneous, I would like to offer a way of thinking about prospects and customers that we use in our work.

Prospects can be:

- Potential buyers who have never heard of your company
- Buyers who know of you, but have not yet chosen to buy from you. Perhaps you gave them a proposal, but didn't get the work
- Former customers who know you and have bought from you, but left you for any number of reasons, and whom you would like to win back.

We define customers as:

- Brand new – just came on board so you're in the honeymoon stage with them.
- Long term, loyal – you have lengthy, solid relationships with them and might even be invited to their children's weddings.

- Come and go:

  - Price Shoppers – Buyers who have little or no regard for who they buy from as long as they can evaporate your margins.
  - Bounce Backs – Those customers who leave you for someone else and bounce back to you because the "grass wasn't greener," and you now have to fix the issues that the other vendor bestowed on these "come and go" customers.

- Hybrids – Combinations of Price Shoppers and Bounce Backs. For example, customers who buy from you and from your competitors, but the amount they buy varies from time to time.

Each of the above categories offers opportunities. Frequently, we discover that a company may have one pitch book or one sales presentation that they use for all prospects and customers. We have come to realize that companies that fully understand the differences in their prospects' and customers' buying criteria, *and adjust accordingly,* score the highest returns on their sales efforts.

Our research shows that the disparity between prospects' and customers' buying criteria can be stunning. Let me give you a couple of quick examples.

A client of ours that sells dental insurance found that their former customers valued the *number of dentists available* more than either their existing customers or pure prospects valued those attributes. The insurer revamped their sales messages to that slice of customers to be more relevant, in order to address what *they* valued.

VNA of Florida, a home health agency, learned that their prospects – doctors who referred patients to home healthcare agencies – wanted to send their patients to an organization that *accepted virtually all health insurance coverage.* On the other hand, the agency's existing customers valued *good communication with the agency* over the fact that they *accepted all insurance.* Apparently, the existing referring docs had their specific needs for insurance coverage met. But doctors who had not yet referred patients to the agency needed assurance of a wider breadth of insurance coverage before they would recommend the agency. If, in their sales messages, the agency simply touted their communication capabilities, they would not have moved the needle for those prospective doctors who were not yet referring patients to them. Once the agency's messages became relevant, their revenues soared.

WHY IT MATTERS

It's essential to continually know what your prospects and your customers want and need so you can be relevant. If you don't, you will have a tough time convincing them not to buy from someone else.

For example, prospects may initially decide to buy from you because of your product's brand or financing options. However, once they use your products and become existing customers, their buying criteria may change. They may continue to do business with you because of your reliability, prompt deliveries, top-notch service, product durability, or the fact that you stand behind everything you sell.

Knowing precisely what each of your customer categories prize will help you:

- Make the wisest investments.
- Give your entire team clearly defined goals.
- Deliver the sharpest, most relevant, most productive sales messages.

Most companies act as if the path to the bullseye is the same for their entire market. Sometimes it is, but more often it's not.

In our work, we've found countless reasons why prospects' and customers' buying criteria differ. The examples and case histories that follow are a sampling of some of the scenarios we've experienced. My hope is that they will show you that differences do exist and will motivate you to examine whether your own prospects and customers have different requirements when they buy. If they do, find the best way to send your sales messages to each group.

WARNING – In business, change is a constant; the needs and wishes of prospects and customers vary over time. New priorities can be caused by numerous variables including time, world economic conditions, political changes, climate, industry development, and location. Therefore, the survey results reported in our examples should be considered in relation to a number of factors, including the time the surveys were conducted, the companies' industries, geography, and the economic atmosphere at the time. Be careful not to assume that you will get the same results with your own customers and prospects.

PROSPECTS DON'T KNOW YOU YET

There is a best-kept secret in New England. The Institute for Trend Research (ITR) is a highly respected New Hampshire firm that tracks and analyzes economic trends. ITR is by far one of the best forecasters on the planet. I can say that unequivocally because I have been following them and their forecasts for over fifteen years. They have amazing accuracy and a unique philosophy and model for forecasting trends. They present to associations and CEO groups nationally and internationally.

Since many of my clients and I have been fans of ITR for years, I was delighted when the Institute asked me to help them determine what their competitive advantages were, relative to their prospects and customers' top preferences. My partner and I journeyed up to beautiful New Hampshire to meet with Alan and Brian Beaulieu, partners and twin brothers with the ability to give economic trends more flavor than any television talking head. The Beaulieu brothers have a gift of being both brilliant in their craft and the ability to deliver dry trend data with comedic relief. In other words, they have a much-needed sense of humor, rarely found in "numbers" guys.

For our visit they pulled together their entire team: brilliant, young B-school analysts and support staff. We worked hard all day. We uncovered scores of potential competitive advantages, and then we designed their customer and prospect survey to determine which were relevant.

When the research results came back, the ITR team discovered that their existing customers prized *on-time delivery* of data more than did their prospects, who had not yet come to rely on the receipt of that valuable information. ITR's prospects wanted more *communication* with the company than did existing clients. The customers had come to realize that the ITR's research was so complete and easy to understand that they didn't need additional communication. Prospects, however, unfamiliar with ITR's work, wanted assurances that they would have access and communication when they needed it.

While more often than not customers' and prospects' hot buttons differ, occasionally they are the same. In this case both groups valued knowing ITRs *historic accuracy rates* with their trend forecasts. As we always tell clients, unlike a mutual fund, in business, "past performance is the best indicator of future performance."

As I mentioned, ITR has great accuracy with forecasting; I was witnessing it year after year. The only thing missing was for ITR to go revisit their past forecasts and calculate their own accuracy rate. After we left New Hampshire on our second visit when we revealed these findings, Brian and Alan and staff decided to invest whatever resources were needed to calculate their own forecast accuracy rate.

It turned out that they were tracking at about 97.8 percent for pre-recession years. But when the recession hit, with all the worldwide uncertainty they slipped a bit, dropping to 94.7 percent. Well, I don't know about you, but if I am to make bets on my company, whether or not to invest in inventory, staff, training, new products, etc., I would be *happy* with 94.7 percent accuracy to guide my decisions. Wouldn't you?

Now ITR provides clients and prospects their trend accuracy to ensure they build confidence and remove risk in the buying decision. They sell all of their trends in a remarkable newsletter, as well as offering one to one consulting services. Their growth rate is accelerating as more and more organizations and associations learn the power of their accurate forecasting capability.

HIGHER STANDARDS

Professional Compounding Centers of America (PCCA), is a Houston, Texas, based organization that provides fine chemicals, equipment, consulting services and technical support to independent compounding pharmacies. If a patient needs a medication of an unusual strength, or in a different dosage form, or one that is no longer commercially available, a compounding pharmacy can work with the patient and prescriber to customize the medication to fit the patients needs. Pharmacy compounding has allowed many pharmacists to find their niche as medication problem-solvers. A drawback of the "one size fits all" nature of many mass manufactured medications is that those products may not meet some patient's needs. Before multinational pharmaceutical companies dominated the market, all medications were compounded. Over the past few decades compounding has experienced a renaissance as more people have come to recognize that a pill or capsule may not be the best way to take in medication. Plus, the technology has advanced to the stage that the delivery of medication can be tailored to an individual's unique needs. Can you get your two-year-old to swallow a pill? Would it be easier to give him or her a medicated lollipop?

Over the years, PCCA has enjoyed a strong relationship with their customers, which include almost four thousand independent compounding pharmacies worldwide that personalize medications for patients. Those customers know and are highly satisfied with the products and services PCCA supplies. However, pharmacies that PCCA had not served were another story; they knew little about PCCA.

When PCCA decided to expand its markets, they surveyed both pharmacies that had not done business with them (prospects), and their existing member pharmacies (customers), to learn what each group wanted most. The survey revealed that a top priority for three-quarters of PCCA's member pharmacies was *the ability to obtain fine chemicals that exceed USP/NF/BP standards for quality and purity*. In contrast, fewer than half the prospects surveyed said that attribute was as important to them.

A similarly large gap occurred with *availability of staff for consulting*: Seventy percent of PCCA's existing customers valued it highly, as compared to fifty-two percent of the company's prospects. That's a statistically significant difference. Existing customers knew from their experience the importance of *quality* and *consulting services*, but prospects did not. Figure 5-A (opposite) is the partial listing of the survey results.

The United States Pharmacopeia (USP) establishes written standards for medicines, food ingredients, and dietary supplement products and ingredients. These standards are used by regulatory agencies and manufacturers to help to ensure that these products are of the appropriate identity, as well as strength, quality, purity, and consistency.

FIGURE 5-A

PCCA Attributes	Members %	Prospects %
Having a live person, in the U.S., answer phone calls	80	70
The firm's investment in Quality Assurance	74	64
Availability of API's and fine chemicals that exceed USP/NF/BP standards for quality and purity	76	48
Availability of staff for consulting	70	52
Speed of response to questions	60	60
Availability of hotline for critical support	64	42
Breadth and depth of inventory available to order	50	54
Support for the compounding industry and profession	68	34
Same day shipping	54	46
Number of formulations on file	54	42

In many cases, USP doesn't have a standard for a given element such as heavy metals like cadmium, i.e., they don't impose a limit on the element as a contaminant in a formulation. Nevertheless PCCA goes beyond USP standards by testing for heavy metals. PCCA informs customers of their additional testing, and pulls products that contain certain potentially harmful ingredients. As a result, customers (1) learn the limitations of the USP standards, and (2) want higher quality. Most prospects don't know that USP does not limit heavy metal contamination, and think that testing to the USP standard is sufficient. So PCCA educates them and clearly explains the differences that make their services so unique.

Similarly, most compounding pharmacies who order from a large supplier (read, warehouse) view that vendor as simply a distributor; they have not experienced PCCA's superb consulting staff. So they don't even realize what they're missing. The result? The prospects don't value these attributes as highly as the members. PCCA needed to make sure their messages to each market segment were relevant to that segment. PCCA is another company who continues to do very well despite lots of competition.

KEEPING CLIENTS, GETTING MORE

In some areas, experience means a lot. Financial service is a good example. McLean & Partners is a global wealth management firm based in Calgary, Canada that manages nearly $1 billion for high-net-worth individuals, family trusts, and not-for-profit corporations. The minimum portfolio the firm will handle is $1 million.

Calgary is Canada's Houston – a boomtown thriving on the oil and gas industry. This city, which started as an outpost for the Royal Canadian Mounted Police, is now Canada's third largest city with a metropolitan area population of more than a million people. Calgary attracts more than three million tourists annually including those who visit every July for the internationally celebrated Calgary Stampede.

On October 2, 2008, my consultants and I traveled to Calgary to work with McLean & Partners. The date is significant. Our timing couldn't have been worse; on that day the stock market hit a new bottom and left the world wide-eyed and scared. We walked into a consultant's nightmare! How would the wealth managers at McLean respond to this market's plunge?

When we took the McLean partners to dinner that night to watch shocked wealth managers get their breath back over a couple glasses of wine, we were pleasantly surprised. The mood shifted as they accepted the news as a fact of life that we all would have to deal with. As the meal progressed, they even became more optimistic because they knew their investment models and research were sound, and would not take as big a hit as they first thought.

We also wondered if our meeting, scheduled for the next day, would proceed. Although the partners were eager to start their work with us, they asked us to delay the start time until later in the day so they could make some reassuring phone calls to their clients.

When we began our process at noon, we were very impressed with the mood and the focus of the firm's team.

Our experience with this client was one for the books, or at least for this book! Several months later, when we made our return visit to deliver the research findings, another calamity struck. For the first and only time in the history of the Canadian stock market, it experienced a major software glitch that completely shut down the

Toronto Stock Exchange, or TSX. The TSX, Canada's equivalent of the NYSE, is the largest stock exchange in Canada, and seventh in the world by market capitalization. More mining and oil companies are listed on the TSX than any other in the world.

We were beginning to feel like "black widow" consultants. Fortunately, the fact that lightning struck during *both* of our visits didn't hinder our client's participation and contributions to the process.

McLean & Partners learned through our competitive advantage process and their research findings that the firm's existing clients valued *experience of research analysts in selecting investments* more than prospects valued that attribute. I guess when money is actually on the table, investors care more about analysts' experience.

McLean decided to act on the differences between prospects' and customers' buying criteria. First, the firm delivered clear messages to their existing customers to help ensure their retention. Here's what the firm's website now states:

- Our private client advisors have an average 17 years experience, and have navigated client wealth through good, bad, and indifferent markets.
- Our research team narrows the field of over 60,000 equities worldwide to a high conviction portfolio of less than 70 stocks. The research team consists of five professionals from North America, Europe and Asia, collectively speaking six languages.

McLean sent a loud, clear message that their people were experienced and had been around the track.

Then the partners decided to invest more time, effort and resources educating prospects on why their research analysts' experience correlated so highly to successful portfolio management. Their standard practice was to personally visit the majority of the companies they invested in to see those businesses first hand, to interview management, and get deeper insights. But they never said so to prospects. Now they do.

For most of us, staying in the market or increasing our investments during the height of the recession often felt like we were playing Russian roulette with a fully loaded gun. The odds seemed to be overwhelmingly stacked against many companies and industries. However, McLean & Partners was able to build their business during those dark times because they learned how to reach new investors and grow the existing, core investors they served by delivering different, and relevant, sales messages.

SOFTWARE FOR TRUCKERS

We also came across differences in what prospects and customers want most in our work with McLeod Software. Since 1985, McLeod has been offering trucking software solutions, and their product line now extends to shippers, freight brokerages, and freight and carrier managers. They alleviate the need for their customers to write their own software, with the attendant IT infrastructure and staff that requires. McLeod's software delivers more value for their customers' business than anything most of them could ever hope to write or develop on their own. McLeod's information systems range from dispatch to imaging, from financial systems to regulatory, and from fuel optimization to driver hiring. They have a base of over 550 customers in North America, and employ more than 190 professionals, most of whom are software developers.

McLeod is headquartered in Birmingham, Alabama, and operates regional offices with training facilities in Salt Lake City, Utah and Downers Grove, Illinois. Birmingham is a transportation center and an ideal location for a trucking software company. The largest city in Alabama, it has a metro population of over a million and is home to over 40,000 businesses. Birmingham blossomed and grew because it was the crossroads of two of the nation's major railroad systems.

Although CEO Tom McLeod's company has been delivering IT to trucking firms for over twenty-five years, as more competitors entered the field, McLeod's offerings became more and more commoditized. Tom wanted to overcome this commoditization.

McLeod commissioned a survey of both customers and prospects among truckers and brokers. The research found that the most important feature for trucking company owners was *continuous support of software* without having to change it out completely every few years. One hundred percent of the *customers* surveyed said that they wanted their software provider to continue to support older versions of their software. The reason for their unanimous response was that, like many software providers, McLeod gives users the capability to add new functionality as McLeod develops it. For example, for their LoadMaster Dispatch Software, customers can add up to forty additional modules and ninety mature and fully tested off-the-shelf integration products. What customers did not want was built-in obsolescence that would force them to pay for all-new software.

When asked the same question, only eighty-six percent of the *prospects* surveyed put *continuous support of software* at the top of their lists. While eighty-six percent is a high number, it should be noted that in attribute testing, a fourteen percent difference is a significant amount. In the software industry, support is not always so extensive, and some companies terminate their support after a specified time. Intuit, for example, stops providing support for QuickBooks after three years. So if you want continuous support, you have to buy the new version. McLeod doesn't do this. Providing continuous software support gives McLeod a big competitive advantage and their customers appreciate its value. But since prospects had not used McLeod's products, they could not appreciate the importance of continuous support of legacy software and the money it saves an organization over time.

A similar gap occurred with the answers given on *call response times*. Ninety percent of the customers surveyed considered the promptness of responses to their phone calls important, compared to seventy-six percent of those prospects questioned. McLeod's data management team can manage and perform scheduled database maintenance and any administration tasks for any customer, on a spot basis or as an ongoing service. Their professional services team has years of experience helping customers with disaster recovery events and business continuity planning services. But prospects have no way of knowing this, unless, of course, McLeod tells them. And if they don't even know the service is available, how can they value it?

REASONS FOR DIFFERENCES

Sometimes the reasons for the differences in prospects' and existing customers' perspectives are quite apparent. For example, when your customers have experience with your company and focus on a particular attribute, say *on-time delivery, product quality,* or *the promptness of response to calls,* they may rank it higher than prospects who have not had the same experience. Customers may have come to depend on your unwavering ability to deliver and have built their organizations' processes in reliance of that attribute.

Often prospects that have no familiarity with you simply need to be educated on the relevance of particular attributes that you bring to the table. You have to show them how the impact of the items you deliver can improve their outcomes.

EXPERTS IN VOLATILITY

Trican Well Service, Ltd. provides pressure-pumping services and solutions to energy industries on four continents. Like McLean & Partners, the company is headquartered in boomtown Calgary. Trican provides a comprehensive array of specialized services to optimize the recovery factor of oil and gas wells during their entire life cycle. Trican is a world leader in new technologies for cementing, coiled tubing, acidizing, nitrogen, fracturing, reservoir characterization, microseismic fracture mapping, industrial cleaning, and pipeline services. They also provide technical expertise, products, and equipment. The company's pressure pumping and industrial services operations are focused in Canada and the United States, as well as in Russia, Kazakhstan, Algeria, Saudi Arabia, and increasingly in other parts of the world.

The company faces a unique combination of major challenges. First, they serve companies in the volatile energy market, where prices constantly fluctuate. When energy prices are high, everyone wants Trican's goods and services. When they're depressed, no one can afford them. Trican also faces tons of intense competition from well-established industry giants, hungry start-ups, and everything in between. Other companies are always trying to grab a share of its business. In addition, some of Trican's business is seasonal, because equipment that they have developed and currently lease for use in Canada's tundra can only operate when the ground is hard frozen, usually November through April.

When prospects and customers were surveyed, one of the top attributes – employee *knowledge, experience, or certifications of employees* – had a twenty percent spread. Eighty-six percent of prospects valued it, compared to sixty-six percent of customers, which is a major difference. Management knew the reason for this wide gap. In the previous few years, some of Trican's competitors had made all sorts of promises to get contracts that they couldn't fulfill. These competitors had large employee turnover so they assigned inexperienced people to critical jobs. The employees' inexperience and lack of knowledge made it impossible for them to solve their customers' problems. Trican was able to capitalize on this difference by clearly emphasizing the experience of their people: "Trican's Canadian technical staff is comprised of seventy technologists, chemists, engineers, geologists, and research Ph.D.'s, who have filed over twenty-six patents and twelve research papers in the past three years."

Trican's customers may not have rated *knowledge, experience, or certifications of employees* as highly as prospects because they were used to working with Trican's highly skilled technical staff, so they took it for granted. When an attribute becomes a given, it's expected to be a part of whatever is delivered. So it's often not rated as highly as something that is not usually received. We suggested another possibility: It may have been that since Trican's knowledge, experience, and qualifications were clearly the best, prospects who had not worked with company expertise offered by Trican, had been forced to hire their own experts to compensate for the lack in their own suppliers.

While Trican immediately recognized the reason for the prospect-customer spread, that's not always the case. We don't always know why prospect-customer differences exist. Nevertheless, when statistically valid research shows that differences do exist, smart sales-people, and intelligent companies, capitalize on that knowledge.

Trican has experienced extraordinary growth in the past few years. They told us that learning what their customers and prospects valued has allowed them to adjust better to serve them. Trican focused their growth plans and marketing on the top three attributes in each case.

RELEVANCE IN TIME

As I wrote in Chapter One, in business change is constant, and it frequently comes at breakneck speed. Therefore, businesses, like marriages, need tweaking from time to time. Some need some serious adjusting in order to remain relevant. The easiest, most foolproof way for businesses to learn when and what to change is by asking their customers – by going to the source, to their market, to those to whom they want to sell, and asking them what they value most. Businesses, unfortunately, do this about as often as spouses ask each other what they want: clearly not often enough.

Changing times and conditions affect what buyers prefer; they create trends and cycles that businesses must understand in order to remain relevant. When the great recession of 2008 took hold, survey respondents in all kinds of industries reported that in making buying decisions, suddenly their top priority was *financial security*. Before the downturn, *financial security* rarely ranked in the top five. *Quality* and *measured outcomes* topped the charts.

During the recession, inventories dropped substantially in many industries. Consequently, issues have arisen that have caused the greatest needs of prospects and customers to change. Many companies now tell us that *on-time delivery* has become of primary importance to them, probably because it's harder and harder to come by. When I recently ordered a set of simple shutters for sliding doors, I was promised that I would have them in six weeks. That was bad news. Six weeks just to get shutters? Then they didn't arrive for three months! When a business relies on an order from another business and it's plagued with problems and delays, the impact is far more serious than my waiting a few additional weeks for shutters for my home.

HOME HEALTH CARE

VNA of Florida, the home health care agency we discussed several pages back, had done double-blind market research five years ago, and had learned that the most important attribute was *patient outcomes*. Their first-level customers were the doctors who referred patients to them. VNA got very good at describing their success with patients, and increased revenues at a record rate for the forty-year old company.

Fast forward four years. During this time they had hired new people, the message had begun to slip, and they began losing market share. They decided, wisely, that things may have changed, and commissioned a new study. This time the CEO and his team learned that what their physician customers valued most was *quality of communication between the agency, patient, family, and doctor*. The doctors wanted to know the status of their patients in real time. My client thought this was good news, since they were one of the only agencies providing nurses and care managers with handheld computers who could update a patient's progress while on a home visit.

But then the study asked respondents which home healthcare agency they thought was best at communication. The bad news was that my client came in eighth out of twelve companies who competed with him.

Without so much as blink, the CEO jumped up and headed for the door. As he was leaving I said, "Hey Don, where are you going?"

He responded by saying, "I am going to tell my HR director to get a search going right away for a manager of communications. I dropped that position a few years ago. Big mistake – it has clearly come back to bite us."

Without that competitive intelligence this company would have gone on blindly sliding down the scale in the eyes of its customers, because what was most relevant had changed over time.

Ten months after this finding, they had recaptured most of the lost market share.

A NEW GENERATION

Let me give you more examples of how relevance can change over time. The world of rental apartment construction is pretty straightforward – build a well-designed, well-constructed building in a good location, and wait for the renters to arrive. Although that formula still works, the meaning of "well-designed" is changing because, as the Wall Street Journal reported (May 6, 2011), a rental construction boom is underway to accommodate the new generation of renters who are leaving home and hitting the rental market. These new renters want different things, so apartment designs are changing. "Echo Boomers," the generation born in the late 1980s to early 1990s, grew up with a higher level of material comfort, often going on vacation with their parents to nice resort hotels. Now that they're graduating from school and leaving home, these young renters want apartments that are less private and more communal – less like stacks of individual units, and more like high-end resorts. They want large communal spaces where they can hang out and entertain.

Many newly constructed apartments are getting smaller. New one-bedroom apartments now average 750 square feet, compared to 900 square feet in the late 1990s, and feature combined living/dining spaces. Developers are thinking about making them even smaller. Instead of big bedrooms and formal dining rooms, this new generation of apartment hunters are willing to trade smaller private spaces in exchange for higher quality public amenities like pools, communal kitchens, movie rooms, fitness centers, and large common areas where they can entertain and socialize with their friends and neighbors.

Apartment developers have done their customer research. They know what their generation of customers want in an apartment. So they're delivering new offerings that are relevant to the changing concept of what an apartment should be. Other enterprising companies are also trying to make their offerings more relevant by bringing them up to date. Here are some examples:

Wristwatches. Fewer young people are wearing wristwatches. They think they don't need a watch when they have a cell phone. So watchmakers are trying to recapture young consumers by being more relevant and reinventing the wristwatch. HP and Fossil have teamed up on a new wristwatch that has wireless internet and Bluetooth capability that alerts the wearer when email, Facebook, or Twitter messages arrive. The idea is to make the wristwatch more relevant, more than just a niche product for telling time.

Fast food. McDonald's Happy Meals have become healthier. The fast-food leader now includes apple slices and smaller French fry portions in its kids' meal boxes. The change reduced calories in the most popular Happy Meals by twenty percent. McDonald's said that the change was made in response to customers' requests for healthier choices, but others feel the move was caused by pressure from government initiatives to reduce childhood obesity. Either way, McDonald's changed in order to be more relevant.

Not to be outdone, Burger King has jumped on the healthy-food bandwagon. In its newest ad, the King has been banished while tomatoes and avocadoes hold court. Health-conscious menu items like the California Whopper, which is garnished with guacamole, are also featured.

Arby's, the fast-food chain known for roast beef sandwiches, is trying to latch onto the growing trend toward eating healthier foods. Arby's had been late in offering a lower cost menu to recession-weary eaters, and lost significant market share to the 'dollar menus.' They didn't stay relevant. Its new marketing campaign tells the world, "Arby's. It's Good Mood Food; exciting tastes you can feel good about . . . every day." The campaign targets "Balance Seekers," busy people who want fast food but not the guilt that often comes with eating it.

Automobiles. BMW is making a huge investment in a new vehicle: an electric car. The 170-horsepower Active E will run for one hundred miles per charge and use no gas, only electricity. Until now, BMW prided itself on being strictly a luxury automaker that concentrated on producing its Ultimate Driving Machines. However, it is now trying to be more relevant and changing with the times. BMW has joined a number of lower-priced car manufacturers in betting that growing numbers of car buyers will change direction and buy more economic eco-friendly cars.

Cruise lines. The old-style egalitarianism on cruise ships may soon be lost at sea. To hold on to some big-spending customers and get them to spend more, several cruise lines are revamping their long-standing policies and offering a more exclusive experience.

Customer research revealed that suite passengers – those paying top dollar for the most lavish accommodations – were dissatisfied with the crowds, the lines, and the quality of ships' amenities. In response, some lines decided to create "ships within a ship" to give these big-spending customers a truly exclusive experience. Now, for a premium, high rollers can get upgraded suite accommodations with VIP perks such as exclusive luxury pool decks, twenty-four-hour butler service, priority bookings for spa treatments, higher quality meals, and complimentary cocktails.

Twitter. This online service that lets people post short, 140-character public messages ("tweets") is only six years old, but it's changing with the times to be more relevant. Although Twitter claims to have two hundred million users, many are not very active and many consider the service a home for online "noise" and celebrity chatter.

So Twitter is taking action to become more relevant to a broader audience. It's developing new ways for first-time users to quickly see how the service works. By highlighting a short list of highly relevant tweets from people in the users' immediate geographic areas, new users can see the latest updates from personalities, politicians, bands, or other Twitter users who interest them, as soon as they sign on. This will make Twitter more accessible and relevant because people will be able to quickly see dialogs in their area, and immediately connect to those that are relevant to them.

For experienced users, Twitter is making it easier for them to sift through all postings. They can find what's relevant to them without having to scroll through the endless messages that are posted in chronological order. Finally, Twitter is purchasing a startup that makes a tweet management platform so its power users – those who constantly send lots of tweets – can monitor their social media in real time and in a single, concise view that's easier to read.

Airlines. Passengers on Virgin America and Southwest Airlines will soon be able to download videos and audios in-flight on their personal devices. Lufthansa and Condor, the German charter airline, currently offer these services. These moves are designed to accommodate passengers who have shown a growing preference to get entertainment on their own electronic devices. The airlines plan to charge for the services – no surprise there! – which will bring in additional revenues.

Virgin America's system will give passengers the options of watching films and TV shows or listening to music from the airline's library. Passengers who cannot finish watching a movie will be able to take it "to go."

"If you're standing still in this place, you're going backwards," says Virgin America CEO David Cush. "We could stand pat and let them catch up, or we can push the envelope."

The bottom line is that customer preferences change fast, and businesses must adapt. Your business can adapt better and more quickly when you know what your customers really want. Then you can design offerings that fit ideally with your customers' needs and goals.

Don't guess what your marketplace wants. So that you can get the facts and stay relevant, at least once a year invest in double-blind research of both your customers and your prospects. Discover where you actually have competitive advantages and where you may have disadvantages. The ROI will be exponential.

DIFFERENT FOLKS,
DIFFERENT STROKES

Some of us instinctively know that prospects and customers value different things, but often we deliver the same sales pitch to both. When we want to keep existing customers and/or sell them more goods or services, have we tailored our communications to be more specific to their perspective? Have we offered to provide what they really want?

Explore this question with your salespeople. Ask them to list the differences in sales messaging they currently deliver to prospects versus those they make to existing customers. Is there a meaningful difference, and what is each pitch based on? Is it feedback, or is it their intuition, perception, or experience in the market-place? Intuition and perception can be on the mark, but not everyone has the best perception skills. Therefore, companies' teams often come up with mixed bags of messaging.

- Do you sell your company the same way to customers and prospects? Do you use the same message to convince customers to *stay* with you that you use to convince prospects to *start* buying from you?
- Are your sales pitches consistent with your marketing materials? Do your salespeople diss your web site or brochure by saying, "They're out of date"? (And, are they?) What kind of message does that send to the listener?

- Have you kept up with changes in your market-place? For example, does *on time* mean the same thing now as it did five or ten years ago? Or does it now mean *just in time*?
- Have your customers and prospects changed in what they want most from you? Whether the recession is over, or just the "new normal," the fear of a supplier going under may be receding, and financial stability is no longer the most critical need. Now maybe they want to be sure you can keep up with their rapidly changing supply chain needs.

Sometimes prospects and customers do, in fact, value the same things. However, it is critical for you to determine if this is the case for each of your target markets. When your prospects value something very different from what your existing customers value, make sure to be relevant to each. If you don't, it could impact your close rates.

CHAPTER 6

Relevant Selling Defines Differences in Buying Criteria for Each Target Market and Each Level of Customer

Most Use One Broad Brush for All

WE'VE SEEN THAT PROSPECTS OFTEN NEED different marketing messages than existing customers. Let's drill down a little deeper and discuss how levels of customers and different target markets impact your marketing messages.

In their marketing, companies often use one broad brush when they try to sell their goods and services to different target markets and different levels of customers. Although some of your target markets or customer levels may place a high value some of the same items, they seldom agree on the same top four or five attributes. And it's even rarer for them to prioritize those attributes in the same order. For example, in my own consulting practice, similar to many organizations, there are three distinct target markets that we serve:

Fortune 500 companies. They often look to us for an objective, new process to ignite creative thinking and motivate their teams.

Mid-sized companies. They value the same thing as *Fortune* 500 companies in hiring a consulting firm but also want some disciplines such as designing the market research based on their newly discovered competitive advantages. They count on us to distill their objectives because they have little or no experience in that area and want that guidance.

Small companies. They look for turnkey marketing and sales messaging. They want our experience with their industry and sector. In fact they want it all, as they often have either no marketing department or a very limited one.

To convert prospects to customers in all three target markets requires us to sell relevantly to each of them, based on what they are seeking. Many companies try a one-size-fits-all sales approach. They say, "Here's what we have to sell; we hope it fits your needs." Your clients/ customers will likely breakdown into similar groupings.

Knowing what each group values is paramount to knowing how to sell them.

We define *Target Market* as a group of customers who are likely to choose a particular supplier of a product or service, for a particular reason. We define *Level of Customer* as the different individuals who have some say in the choice: decision makers, influencers, evaluators, executors, and end users, for example.

Figure 6-A illustrates these two concepts graphically.

FIGURE 6-A

Target Markets and Levels of Customers

Target Markets:
A group of customers of a type—by demographics—considered likely to buy a particular product

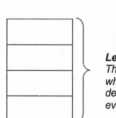

Levels of Customers:
The different types involved in or who can influence the sale— decision makers, influencers, evaluators, executors, end users

A seafood company might sell to the target markets and levels of customer shown in Figure 6-B.

FIGURE 6-B

Target	Target	Target
Restaurants	Supermarkets	Cruise Lines

	Levels of Customer	
Food Buyer	Home Office	Purchasing Manager
Chef	Store Manager	Chef
Consumer	Consumer	Consumer

There is another aspect to levels of customer that will be familiar if you sell your product or service through a middleman. These include wholesalers, distributors (both warehousing and drop ship), insurance brokers, and real estate agents. You can probably add another dozen to the list.

BIG FIVE, REVISITED

Big Five Tours & Expeditions, the tour operator that you first met in Chapter One, markets to two levels of customer: (1) travel agencies that sell Big Five tours to travelers, and (2) travelers who experience the company's adventure tours. We designed survey questionnaires for each level of customer, and Big Five commissioned double-blind surveys of both groups. The objective was to identify what each group wanted most from a tour operator.

As you learned in Chapter One, Big Five's *awards*, the attribute the company promoted most, came in dead last with travel agents and next to last with travelers. And both groups said that the fact that Big Five was a *longstanding family operation* didn't influence their buying decision one bit. We see this incorrect assumption in many companies. They want to proudly tout their decades in the business, but it has little or no influence in buying decisions according to most research studies. Remember Lehman? AIG?

The attribute that travel agents actually valued most was *financial stability*. The fact that agencies prized *financial stability* made sense to us, because agencies don't want their clients to spend lots of money on a trip and then have their tour operator go belly up. If a travel agent booked a traveler on an elaborate journey with a tour operator, and then before the trip the tour operator went under, it would be a disaster for the agent. The agent would be left holding the bag and have to deal with the fallout.

The reason that this issue made the top of the list is because it is not theoretical. Some travel agencies have been burned by bankrupt operators. And so while to the general public the problem may seem obscure, it looms large to travel agents.

When we discussed this finding with Big Five, they gave us another twist. Twice in recent memory a travel agent had called them, horrified because travelers who took other operators' trips were stranded far away when their tour guides disappeared because the tour operator had not paid them. In each case, Big Five came to the rescue and got the travelers through their journey. No wonder *financial stability* was so important to those agents!

Two items tied for second place with the travel agencies surveyed: *the tour operator's responsiveness to complaints* and their *attention to detail*. Although Big Five was *financially stable, responded promptly to complaints,* and *paid great attention to details,* they didn't tout any of those qualities because they thought that they were too obvious to highlight in their messages. The tour operator incorrectly assumed that their competitors also performed those items well; they assumed they were "givens" in the industry. This is also a mistake many companies make.

Travel agencies also reported that *the tour operator's prompt payment of commission* was of great importance to them. Big Five reviewed their records and found that ninety-two percent of the time, they issued commission checks to agencies within fifteen days of the travelers' *departure* on their tour; their competitors' standard practice was to pay the commission thirty days after the travelers *returned*. Again, Big Five hadn't promoted what was relevant: their record of prompt payment to agents. Now they make sure to remind agencies how quickly they pay compared to other tour operators. Note how this competitive advantage statement also speaks to Big Five's financial stability.

When we surveyed the next level of customer – the travelers who purchased high end adventure tours – none of the items that Big Five highlighted in their sales pitches topped the travelers' lists; none of the attributes that were most important to the agencies topped the travelers' lists either. The number one priority for travelers was *level of knowledge of destinations by tour operator's staff*. Then came *having a live person in the U.S. answer their phone calls,* and *tour operator's speed of response to questions.* Although Big Five excelled in each of these areas, they neglected to emphasize how well they delivered them. Now they do.

Take a look at Big Five's website (www.bigfive.com). Their home page addresses the top concerns of travelers. Under the heading, "Five Reasons To Travel With Big Five Tours & Expeditions," the company lists the top attributes that travelers said they prize most. Then facts are cited to support each claim. For example, under item number one, *Level Of Staff Knowledge*, the home page states:

"At Big Five, you are working with one of the most experienced group of individuals in the luxury travel industry. Our Destination Specialists received 900+ hours of on-site and in-office product training in the last 12 months. They are part of a diverse team assembled from 11 countries over 5 continents speaking a combined 10 different languages. Several of our Destination Specialists have been recognized for their expertise, including three who were named on Travel+Leisure's 2009 A-List of Travel Agents."

By learning how the buying criteria of each level of customer differs, and then addressing those differences with specific messages, Big Five has boosted their revenues. New tours in new areas are being offered, and the tour operator has formed strategic alliances with outstanding travel companies in other countries.

In early 2009, at the lowest point in the economic downturn, Big Five surveyed agencies and travelers. At that time, their competitors' revenues had dropped by fifty to sixty percent and some of their rivals went out of business. In September/October 2009, Big Five sent out the new, customer-focused messages that we helped develop. By the end of the year, Big Five had stemmed their losses. In 2010, their profits were up by fifteen percent and the company was in position to make substantial gains in years to come. Last time I checked, Big Five had year-over-year sales increases over forty percent.

DIFFERENT CUSTOMERS, DIFFERENT MESSAGES

I presented a public seminar on creating competitive advantages to a group of mid-sized business owners in Philadelphia. One of the attendees was Ken Baker, the CEO and son of the founder of NewAge Industries. Ken was intrigued when he realized how little he really knew about his company's customers. My partner, Craig Mowrey, was assisting that day and spent extra time guiding Ken through the process. By the end of the day, Ken's frustration was mounting as he became more and more aware that NewAge wasn't getting their sales and marketing messages right. So Ken asked us to come to NewAge's site to help his team.

NewAge Industries started as the dream of Raymond Baker in 1954. That year, this young salesman-turned-entrepreneur purchased a small company that both manufactured and imported metal hardness testers. A year or so later, while on a business trip to England, he found a revolutionary new product that he felt had huge potential in the United States: a clear, nylon-braid-reinforced, flexible PVC hose. It didn't fit the hardness tester business, so he started a second business with this new product, Nylobrade®.

NewAge Industries is now a multi-million dollar manufacturer and fabricator of flexible plastic and rubber tubing and hose. They also supply fittings, clamps, and accessories for a wide variety of industrial and high purity applications. With their sister plant, Colex International, Ltd, of Leicestershire, England, they produce tens of millions of feet of tubing and hose each year. NewAge offers one of the broadest product lines of tubing, hose, and fittings in the U.S., and their custom extrusion and fabrication services are unrivaled.

NewAge has its corporate offices and state-of-the-art

manufacturing center in Southampton, Pennsylvania, about a half-hour north of Philadelphia.

Like several of our clients, NewAge wears two hats: one as a manufacturer and the other as a distributor. As a manufacturer, NewAge has two target markets: (1) Original Equipment Manufacturers (OEMs), the end users of NewAge tubing; and (2) distributors that stock NewAge's products and resell them. Companies that prefer to deal with a supplier that is located in close proximity to their R&D and/or manufacturing facilities, small shops, or those that just need a small amount of tubing, typically buy from distributors. Plus, sometimes larger manufacturers prefer not to stock large quantities of the materials they use. As a distributor, NewAge maintains a sizeable warehouse and is willing to invest in this service when the local distributor cannot.

NewAge needed a better way to talk about their company. Their website and all of their brochures and marketing materials were product focused. They went into great detail about their tubing's quality and specifications, but they didn't promote the company and didn't specifically state what they could do for their customers. NewAge knew that they needed help articulating the benefits that they could deliver to their prospects and customers.

The company also needed assistance in handling the fact that they were a distributor, and that many had the perception that NewAge was competing with the distributors they supplied as a manufacturer. NewAge wanted to find out the top buying criteria of both of their target markets, the OEMs and distributors, so they could improve their messaging and sell more of their products to both markets.

When we met with NewAge at their corporate head-quarters, we asked the executive team members what they thought OEMs wanted most from a company that sells flexible tubing and hoses. According to the staff, the OEMs' number one priority was *product quality*, Number two was *on-time delivery*, followed by *same-day shipping* and *application engineering assistance*. Since NewAge is located near Philadelphia and over half of their customers are in the Northeast, they had stressed the fact that they provide one-day delivery and were convinced that one-day delivery was of great importance to OEMs.

In keeping with our process, we designed a customer research survey for their two target markets. Designing the questions was tricky because of NewAge's status as a manufacturer, a distributor, and a company that sold their goods to other distributors. A number of variables were involved, and NewAge wanted to know how their target markets perceived their own buying patterns.

In the survey, OEMs were asked, "How do you buy goods? Do you buy:

(1) Directly from a stocking (warehousing) distributor?
(2) From a distributor, but have the goods drop shipped

from a manufacturer (the distributor is essentially an order taker)?

(3) Directly from the manufacturer?

(4) From both the distributor and manufacturer?

(5) Some other way?"

The survey found that a third of the OEMs bought directly from manufacturers. Another third bought from both distributors and manufacturers, depending on how quickly they needed the goods and how much they wanted. A quarter bought from a stocking distributor. Although NewAge thought that they did a substantial amount of drop shipping, only three percent of respondents said they bought drop shipments. The company only knew what percentage of their business they drop shipped to end users, not what percentage of the market that represented.

Then the survey asked, "If you're buying from a distributor, what distributor do you use?" Since NewAge sells to distributors and competes against other manufacturers' distributors, they wanted to find out the size of the market and how many competitors they had. The research found that NewAge was in a crowded market: thirty-three different distributors were named, including NewAge.

Thus the groundwork was laid for NewAge to view their buyers as three target markets, each of whom had a different hierarchy of buying criteria: OEMs who buy directly from manufacturers (OEM-Ms in Figure 6-C below); OEMs who buy from distributors (OEM-Ds); and Distributors.

Target market No. 1: - The key attributes for OEM-Ms were *product quality, on-time delivery*, and *responsiveness to complaints* and *accuracy of documentation* [tied].

Target market No. 2: The key attributes for OEM-Ds were *order accuracy* and *on-time delivery* [tied], followed by *customer service calls answered by a person*, and *quick response to complaints. Product quality* was fifth.

Target market No. 3: The key attributes for distributors were *product consistency* and *order accuracy* [tied], followed by *speed of response to inquiries.*

Aggregating the responses shows the commonality among the top attributes:

FIGURE 6-C

Attribute	OEM-M	OEM-D	Distributor
Quality/consistency*	1	5	1
Speed of delivery	2	1	2
Responsiveness	3	4	3
Accuracy	3	1	1

*We view product consistency as an element of quality.

This same knowledge allowed NewAge to tailor their messages to each target market. For example, when they are marketing to OEM-Ds, NewAge can speak *first* about the speed and accuracy of their orders. Obviously that would not be the first message to OEM-Ms; that target market is more concerned about quality of the products. Acting on these subtle distinctions, by marketing what a particular segment values most, is what differentiates good, relevant selling from cliché selling. Knowing these subtle distinctions, *and checking to see if they match a particular customer or prospect by asking appropriate questions*, is what differentiates great salespeople from the also-rans.

Michael Tangreti, Director of Marketing for NewAge, tells me this process have given his team, and the NewAge sales force a whole new way of communicating with their customers and prospects.

In their advertisements, NewAge now states,

"We know how important product quality is to you.

That's why our quality assurance programs are continually monitored and updated, *and* why, over the past six years, we've shipped 99.73% of our products with zero defects."

NewAge doesn't just claim to provide top quality goods, they give impressive, cold, hard, supportive facts. The company cites statistics. They state the exact percentage of the products that they delivered that were defect free. Few manufacturers can substantiate a claim like that.

MULTIPLE MARKETS AND LEVELS

A number of our clients have to weave through long and complex sales processes in order to close sales. Their markets often consist of multiple customer types and further divisions within each customer type. Student Resource Services (SRS) is a company that continually must hack their way through this thicket.

SRS sells student counseling and resource assistance programs to colleges and universities. Their services help students overcome personal barriers that may interfere with their school success, and alleviate issues that may prevent them from completing their education. Since 1990, the company has worked closely with schools to identify at-risk students and get them the help they need to stay in school. SRS, headquartered in St. Louis, Missouri, customizes an approach for each school to ensure the best fit with the school culture and structure.

Here's where it gets complex. SRS contracts with all kinds of post-secondary schools: for-profit and non-profit colleges and universities, trade schools, and online and brick-and-mortar institutions. SRS wanted to increase their sales to for-profit schools and expand their business with not-for-profit schools. Prior to our involvement, SRS thought that their best potential customers were for-profit institutions, so they had concentrated their sales and marketing messages on that target market. Their core message to for-profit educators was that they helped keep at-risk students in school, which kept the schools' money stream flowing.

SRS also wanted us to help them shorten their sales cycle. The sales cycle was often prolonged because SRS struggled to identify the final decision maker (the individual within the organization authorized to buy SRS's services). Since the final decision makers appeared to differ from school to school – it could be the CEO, CFO, President, Treasurer, Dean, or others – SRS often ended up making presentations to employees who didn't seem to pass vital information to decision makers.

Many schools have in-house staffs that run their own student assistance and counseling services, but others outsource those services to firms such as SRS. SRS's perception was that their biggest "competitor" was in-house staff, in that the majority of schools still used a traditional on-site counseling staff for students. So we agreed that these would be the two best target markets to study: those schools that outsource some or all of their student counseling, and those that do it all in-house.

Respondents were asked, "Does your college outsource any mental health counseling or resource services?" Fifty-three percent of the respondents answered yes; forty-seven percent answered no. This fairly even split gave us usable comparisons on what the two target markets valued. The largest differences between those schools who outsourced and those who did not related to two attributes: *call length*, and *references*.

Eighty-seven percent of schools who outsourced highly valued *no quota or limit on call length,* while only sixty-four percent of the in-house cohort valued it highly. SRS explained that many of their competitors did limit the time a counselor was allowed to spend on a call with a student, and/or limited the number of calls from a given school, before they imposed additional fees. So schools that already outsourced their counseling service had likely run into this quota/limit issue and didn't like it.

There was almost a mirror image result on another attribute: *good references from other colleges*. Eighty-five percent of the in-house market valued it highly, but only sixty-six percent of the outsource market did. We spent some time with SRS discussing why this difference might be, but ultimately what mattered to the sales and marketing effort was not the *reason why*, but the *fact of*. In other words, regardless of *why* the in-house market thought more of references from other colleges, the implementation of this knowledge meant a change to SRS's pitch to this market that emphasized *references*. And their pitch to schools that outsource needed to place more emphasis on SRS's absence of call limits.

As with NewAge, knowledge of how the buying criteria of their target markets differed allowed SRS to tailor their messages to address the deliverables of most concern to each market. They could now commence relevant selling.

Another surprise result from the survey was that the top buying priority for prospects and customers was *history of maintaining student confidentiality*, which SRS staff had ranked a lowly thirteenth on the list. Why? SRS management told us that confidentiality was a no-brainer. "It's a given in the industry," they explained. "Something that everyone understood, so it didn't have to be said." So SRS's messages didn't emphasize it.

Confidentiality is not such a given in the industry, SRS later learned. SRS and a competitor were the finalists for a contract with a university, when the university called the competitor to ask a number of questions. The final question was, "If we run into a situation with a student, can you divulge pertinent information that you gathered?" Although releasing such information was almost certainly a violation of both HIPAA (the Health Insurance Portability and Accountability Act) and FERPA (the Family Educational Rights and Privacy Act), the competitor replied it would find a way to get the information out "if the circumstances warranted."

When the university called and asked SRS the same question, they flatly said, "No, it's against regulations to share such information without the student's detailed, written permission."

SRS was awarded the contract. By calling both companies, the university had been doing due diligence; they were checking on a matter of great importance to them.

SRS subsequently learned that their commitment to maintaining confidentiality was a major factor in their receiving the award. And the university's decision verified, and more than paid for, SRS's customer research survey.

We needed to address the issue of who at the schools actually makes the final decision to buy. We designed the customer research survey to track the respondents' titles. The survey specifically asked who considered him or herself to be an influencer or a decision maker in the purchasing process. By a two-to-one margin, the respondents identified themselves as influencers, not decision makers.

We found no logic or consistency in the answers: influencers were CFOs, Presidents and Deans; officers whom you would think could make the final calls.

Ultimately we learned that buying decisions were frequently made by committees, not by individuals, especially in schools who had not previously outsourced counseling. This explained why many C-suite leaders identified themselves as influencers, not decision makers. It also helped SRS understand why they had to make so many seemingly fruitless presentations. The apparent decision makers had no more decision-making authority than a jury foreman. In fact, that's a particularly apt analogy, because these officers usually chaired the committee, i.e., they simply reported the committee's decision.

SRS also gained interesting insight into the buying criteria of these self-proclaimed influencers, compared to the (again, self-proclaimed) decision makers.

One attribute, *willingness to take off-hours calls*, ranked a lowly nineteenth out of twenty-two with decision makers, but a much higher sixth with influencers. SRS understood the reason: many times the in-house counselors were members of the decision-making committee choosing an outsource supplier, and they *liked* the idea of someone else, at a fully staffed, wide awake call center taking those three a.m. calls.

SRS had not known to capitalize on their understanding by emphasizing that capability. Now they say:

"In the past twelve months, 22.3 percent of student calls were taken between 6:00 PM-6:00 AM (Central), or on weekends."

MORE UP AT BATS

A not-for-profit company providing cutting-edge school administration software, hardware, internet services, and professional development programs designed by educators, TIES Education Technology Collaborative also needed to rethink their approach and refocus their messaging. TIES was formed in 1967 as Technology Information Education Services, and is owned by forty-six school districts in Minnesota. When we met them, the organization faced heavy competition from a number of major competitors including SAP and Microsoft.

We visited TIES in Minneapolis in the dead of winter. We had to wade through a foot of snow, and this

Floridian showed up without boots. I remember taking a good slip and fall and hoped it wasn't a precursor to how our engagement with TIES would go. Fortunately it wasn't. Although we had to wade through piles of information, we had no more slip-ups.

TIES sells its "Software as a Service," i.e., cloud-based, and was losing bids to competitors that sold and leased directly to schools. So Executive Director Betty Schweizer wanted to find out how they could increase their sales of the financial software that TIES sold to school districts, and the best way to unveil and sell new software that they developed.

All of TIES' sales messages were product-based. They emphasized the *quality of the software's features* because TIES thought that was what prospective customers wanted.

The results of the TIES double-blind customer research survey showed the respondents were less concerned with the product's bells and whistles than TIES thought. First, they wanted *system reliability and stability,* followed in order by *software specifically designed for schools*, *data security and integrity,* and *ease of compliance with state specific requirements.*

When we reviewed the results with TIES' executives, we pointed out the need for them to refocus their messages and make them more relevant. As a result, TIES' sales pitches are now far less product-feature focused. Instead, they tout the attributes that those surveyed said they wanted most. TIES' new messages also address *ease of transition* because school districts don't change software often, since it's a cumbersome and difficult process. This was important in convincing prospects that the transition was worthwhile.

Below is a sampling of the message that now appears on the TIES website for their finance system (http://www. finance.ties.k12.mn.us):

System reliability and stability

- TIES has achieved better than a 99.6% uptime rate in the past five years.
- TIES has invested over $5 million in infrastructure upgrades in the past five years.

Data security and integrity

- Since its inception, TIES has never had a security breach.
- TIES solution is the only K-12 system that provides a Level 1 PCI-DSS certified and SAS70 type II audited hosting environment.

Software designed specifically for schools

- Focused solely on education technology, TIES is the only ERP system based in Minnesota and owned by Minnesota school districts.
- TIES has designed software exclusively for schools seven years longer than any competitor.

In the past, when TIES responded to requests for proposals, they were eliminated in the early stages of the procurement process because their proposals didn't communicate what was most relevant to their customers. Now, TIES is a finalist in most bids and is receiving more awards. TIES executives feel that their new messaging has made the difference.

LAZY OR LASER FOCUSED

As described, our research has proven that each target market and level of customer buys for different reasons. Ask yourself and your team the following questions.

- How do you segment your target markets now? By the traditional boundaries: size, geography or territory, purchase volume, product line?
- If you were to reorganize them by *what they value most,* how might your segmentation change?
- Do you tout your awards, your business structure (public, private, family), or your longevity? What proof do you have that your customers care?
- How many different *levels of customer* do you have to pitch to make a sale?
- How many are influencers? Decision makers? How do you know? Is that your perception, or theirs?
- Is it possible that some of those you perceive as decision makers are just "jury foremen?" If you answered "yes," how might that impact your presentation to them, either singly, or in a group?
- Do you sell through a middleman? If so, do you also sell directly to your middleman's customers? We're not suggesting you change your business model, but you might see *great* benefit in addressing what your middleman values, because I can guarantee it's not the same as what the end user wants!

CHAPTER 7

Operational Gaps Affect Relevant Selling

Tell Your Own People What's Relevant

I'M NOT REALLY MUCH OF A SPORTS AFICIONADO, but decades ago I dated an offensive guard for the New York Giants. On football teams, offensive linemen are the unsung heroes who do unglamorous and difficult work. Although they take the hard blows, sacrifice their bodies, and anchor their teams, they're rarely the biggest stars. Yet without their strength, skill, and solid focus, the more heralded stars – the quarterbacks and receivers – would never put points on the board. Getting those points on the board is always a team effort.

Companies are teams, and every employee is an

essential member of the team. Each employee, even the unsung heroes, plays a specific and critical role. Research frequently reveals who the unsung heroes are in the company; it might be the department you least expect.

Employees are frequently so busy and so focused on their particular tasks that they don't realize how the day-to-day work they perform affects the relevance of their company's sales and marketing. They don't realize how their work fits in with other employees' efforts, and how all the different pieces come together in the final product to pave the way for more sales and higher close rates.

If the production team and the sales team operate with different objectives or disparate agendas, problems will inevitably arise. Like an engine with a defective fuel injector, the business will run, but it will sputter, use lots of fuel, and get nowhere fast. On the other hand, when everyone knows his or her role, its impact, and how it fits, things will run smoothly, customers will get what they want, and will keep coming back. This is common knowledge in theory, yet not so common in practice, based on our research and experience.

In successful, well-run companies, each person contributes to the whole. Plant managers must understand how product quality and timely deliveries impact sales. They must understand that if delays or defects occur, the sales force can't tell prospects, "For the last three years, we've had 98% on time delivery and less than 1% returns."

Customers want, and are entitled to, consistently

excellent performance; goods or services that they can rely upon every time, not promises that are hit and miss. Buyers don't want excuses; they have their own problems and don't want to hear about yours. They just want:

- What they ordered.
- When it was promised.
- With the quality they expect.

While this concept is fundamental, execution is much more elusive. As Larry Bossidy and Ram Charan wrote in *Execution: The Discipline of Getting Things Done* (Crown Business, 2002), "In its most fundamental sense, execution is a systematic way of exposing reality and acting on it. Most companies don't face reality very well."

Here's reality. Double-blind market research, in which you survey both your customers and your prospects, is also a systematic way of exposing reality. Finding out what they really want, based on a statistic weighting of their actual preferences, cuts through all of the biases of negotiation, of preconceptions, of assumptions, and of posturing.

ON TIME, ERROR FREE

Communication gaps produce disasters. Let me give you an example. A company that manufactured plastic credit cards for financial institutions lost a large client – one of the country's major banks. The manufacturer's sales rep begged the bank for another chance to win the business back, and her persistence paid off. As an incentive, the card manufacturer offered the bank a ridiculously low price: they would do the job at cost. Ultimately, the bank gave in and agreed to give the manufacturer a small order albeit with no margin.

Now, getting another shot was no small feat; even though the company only got a small order from the bank, they got much more – a second chance. Once you lose a customer, the odds of winning them back are heavily stacked against you. Regaining a lost customer can take infinitely more work than it took to get that customer to buy from you in the first place. Trust is tough to rebuild when promises have been broken.

For the bank, the order was a test run to see how well the manufacturer would perform. From the bank's perspective, the manufacturer's price was so low that it had little to lose. However, the manufacturer had lots on the line. As small as the order was, it gave the manufacturer a chance to redeem itself and get a foot back in the door. If the manufacturer performed well, they hoped to earn larger and more profitable orders from the bank.

The bank's key demand was "on time, error free." Unfortunately, the manufacturer's upper management never informed its own production manager how much was at stake! He wasn't told that the company's highest priority was to meet the bank's deadline for delivery.

What he saw was a small order with no profit, so he relegated it to the bottom of his production schedule.

Sure enough, the cards were delivered late. The manufacturer received no further orders from the bank. Had the production manager been told how important the order was to his company, and how to meet the bank's expectations, the story could have ended happily.

BRIDGE THE GAP

Even the brightest, best, and most dedicated workers have difficulty seeing beyond their individual tasks. A few years ago I had the privilege of delivering a keynote address to production managers for the Hoerbiger Group in Vienna, Austria. Hoerbiger is a century-old international manufacturer of compression, automation, and drive technologies. The company is headquartered in Switzerland, has 6,500 employees, and sells products to the gas process industry, to the auto industry, and to machinery and plant construction firms throughout the world.

When I found out that my audience would be production managers, I wasn't sure how they would respond to my talk about competitive advantage. My task was to get past my right-brain marketing-and-sales thought process in order to reach this group of left-brain engineer types. I had to figure out how bridge this gap and connect my message to my audience.

At the beginning of my talk, all I saw was a sea of blank expressions. Their U.S. CEO, Hannes Hunschofsky, is a very bright, outside-the-box thinker, but I could tell these engineers wondered if Hannes had lost his mind when he invited me to speak. As I explained what a competitive advantage is, what it is not, and how companies can uncover their competitive advantages, I saw mostly quizzical looks. I felt like I was telling these brilliant engineers what the three bears had to do with Goldilocks. In my mind, I could hear them saying, "Yeah, so? Why is this important to us? We're not in sales!" They were attentive and polite, but hadn't yet connected my message to their roles. They didn't see how their roles were relevant to sales.

I went on to explain that Hoerbiger had recently commissioned a survey to find out what their customers wanted most in their products and service. That's when some audience members began to stir. Then I informed them of the survey results: their customers wanted *top quality products*, which my audience knew, but they also wanted *on-time delivery* and *shorter lead times,* which my audience did not know. The mood in the room visibly changed. The connection had started.

They understood how valuable each of their roles was to the company. Without their engineering expertise, without their diligent work, Hoerbiger would not have top quality products, one of the competitive advantages that was most important to their customers and prospects.

Then I explained that outstanding engineering was not enough. Although it was essential, irreplaceable, and highly valued (with the engineers, flattery got me everywhere!), it was not the end of the story. There was more. Engineers who managed the plants had an additional role: to support company sales.

How their role related to sales was not intuitive for Hoerbiger's production managers. They were focused on production and didn't give much thought to how their efforts impacted sales, which is a common problem at most companies. Dedicated, hard working people were so involved in their individual areas that they hadn't considered how their work related to other pieces of the puzzle; in this case, sales.

As I pressed on, the group got it. These Hoerbiger production managers immediately understood that the survey findings made good sense. They had an awakening. Engineering can produce quality, but Production produces on-time delivery and shorter lead times. If *Production* doesn't produce, then *Marketing* can't market these competitive advantages and *Sales* can't sell them. Simple.

Hunschofsky told me this work with his team made them look at their products and services in a completely different light. Hoerbiger is built on the pillar of engineering solutions. He said, "We see ourselves as an engineering company, and although we produce products, we take great pride in and focus on our engineering solutions. You helped us see that what is really important to us may not be that important to our customers. Since we were so focused on being an engineering company, we weren't giving enough attention to other items that were important to our customers such as *on-time deliveries* and *reducing lead times*. We weren't providing the complete package that creates great customer satisfaction.

"Since we started focusing on providing the whole package, our global surveys show that we are getting better customer satisfaction ratings. We can connect that improvement to our having closer relationships with our customers, to better understanding their needs, and to our internal efforts to fill all their needs; while still giving them superior products and engineering solutions."

INTERNAL ADJUSTMENTS

Your company may be a great organization that produces fantastic, cutting-edge products, but if you don't know what your prospects and customers want, you can't effectively communicate internally and externally. Internally, you can't build operations that provide what your markets want, and externally, you can't come up with sales messages that convince prospects and customers to buy. The Studebaker Avanti, Apple's Newton, and the original Volkswagen beetle are classic examples of products that didn't do well because they were before their time. Or were they really victims of misalignment between companies and their customers?

Were they examples of trying to sell something irrelevant to the market? Remember, "not yet relevant" is still irrelevant!

Some companies get stuck in ruts. They keep pushing the same old buttons and are mystified when they no longer work, but they keep on pushing them nevertheless. Instead of examining their operations and finding what's wrong, they don't change. With heads in sand (what an old boss of mine used to call full-blown ostrich syndrome), they keep on doing what always worked and hope that they're just in a slump that will end soon. Remember the definition of insanity?

Fortunately, companies can discover their problems, make adjustments, rebound, prosper, and grow. Let me tell you about one.

SALUMI, ANYONE?

Volpi Foods is a family-owned global food corporation and America's oldest and most prestigious manufacturer of salumi: handcrafted, authentic Italian meat products. (No, that's not a typo. "Salumi" is the correct word for the category of Italian meats; salami is a specific type of salumi. Who knew?) Company president Lorenza Pasetti comes by her chops organically. Her father, Armando Pasetti, was the second salumiere, or salumi-making expert, to head Volpi Foods, after his uncle John Volpi started the company in 1902. Lorenza is the third.

Volpi one of a handful of U.S.-based salumi artisans that provide European-inspired cured meats to national, regional, and specialty supermarket chains. Volpi is the only U.S. manufacturer that uses 100% fresh meat. Their products also contain the finest ingredients and are cured, dried, and aged in the traditional Italian way. Their product line includes salami, wine salami, prosciutto, capocolla, coppa, pancetta, bresaola, and mortadella. My mouth is watering while I'm writing this!

Volpi competes in a crowded market and battles huge mass producers including household names like Hormel and Boar's Head. Volpi products carry a premium price that reflects their artisanal approach. There are a limited number of stores and chains who would pay extra for, or are willing to allocate the shelf space necessary to support, a high-end specialty meat product. In addition, Volpi requires minimum batch orders, which can hinder individual stores or smaller markets such as wine shops from adding Volpi to their product line. The result is that Volpi is likely chasing the same customer set as most of the mass-market providers in the industry.

The Volpi managers met us in their conference room at the company processing plant in St. Louis, MO, where we sat surrounded by the aromas of their delectable meats. A few blocks from the plant, the company has a retail store. It's located on "The Hill," the heart of St. Louis' historic Italian neighborhood. Besides providing public access to a local favorite, the store is a retail incubator where Volpi can test their products and get direct feedback from customers. They can also put up posters with their messages to see how they resonate. Volpi lovingly calls the store their "very expensive market research facility." We saw a nice touch in the store: a flag on the wall that's covered with the logos of all the restaurants that buy from Volpi.

Recent trends produced new challenges for Volpi. Although artisanal foods are now in vogue and command a premium price, retailers want the artisan suppliers to meet the same tight deadlines that mass producers meet. As the nation becomes more health conscious, buyers also want foods that contain more natural ingredients and fewer additives and preservatives. And of course, many retailers want to sell their own "brands," known in the trade as private label. It's a market Volpi is asked to serve more and more.

So Volpi decided to explore fertile new sectors. However, before investing heavily in new directions, management decided to shore up their core business and strengthen the company name. So they contacted us to help them improve their messaging, distinguish them from their competition, and create more sales.

When we reviewed Volpi's messages, we noted that they were not appreciably different than those of their competitors. Volpi heralded the company's long tradition of following time-tested methods, using the finest ingredients, and taking the extra time and care to produce the best-tasting products. These were the same claims their competitors made.

Three of the top six attributes revealed by the customer research survey were elements of customer service: *accuracy of order fulfillment, on time delivery,* and *processor's ability to resolve issues quickly.*

Volpi believed, and took pride in the fact, that they provided great customer service. Their salespeople work closely with their customers, and the company call center is always at their beck and call. However, Volpi learned that providing what customers want is not the exclusive concern of their customer service department; everyone in the company must be focused, involved, and accountable.

"The survey showed us how important accuracy of order fulfillment was to buyers, which put our production people and our shipping people on notice," President Lorenza Pasetti explained. "Now, they religiously monitor and track all orders because they understand their impact on sales."

When everyone in the company learns what's most important to the company's customers, it's remarkable how well they will strive to meet those needs. Instead of having to rely on promises they hope the company can fulfill, the sales force can tout documented performance. If accuracy of order fulfillment is a highly valued attribute, how much more convincing it is to be able to point to key performance indicators that track exactly that order accuracy.

"We have been able to implement many of the lessons we learned from your process," Pasetti told me. "I call the meeting where we learned the survey results the 'rallying meeting' because we all rallied and came together. The salespeople were the first to attach themselves to the results and run with them. It's been exciting for them. It's also been beneficial for disciplines that we measure internally."

In the past, Volpi couldn't promote their customer service because they didn't have the metrics to support their claims. As we go to press, the company is gathering data, facts and figures, to document their track record to show how well they deliver what their prospects and customers said they want.

Besides tracking how well they provide the services that buyers want most, communications at Volpi have improved. "The clarity we got from the process helped us improve our communication," Pasetti says. "Everyone was engaged in the process and everyone was fully informed of the results, and it made the lines of communication comfortable. We knew that the salespeople would take the survey results and run with them, but we didn't want to lose the momentum that was built internally. That internal momentum is extremely important because it corrals everybody and I don't want to diminish what that momentum can generate. People throughout the company are participating more, they are much more engaged and they want to succeed. They feel that they have a stake in the company's success."

Management now regularly ensures that the staff understands and focuses on what prospects and customers want. They are also factoring the survey respondents' desires into their daily decisions. "I've seen a lot of improvement," Pasetti notes. "I see a lot more enthusiasm and our employees are a lot more engaged. The proof of the pudding has been increased sales."

Relevant selling could now occur because internal staff knew what customers wanted most, and could see their role in delivering on those top attributes.

MAKING THE CONNECTION

So we're not just talking about communications. We're also talking about connecting the dots. Making sure a clear line runs from what the customer demands to where your fulfillment of those demands begins, and who is accountable for that fulfillment. It also involves ensuring that all your employees along the way are clear on the impact they have on your sales force's ability to deliver on their promises. The folks who make it all happen need to be in the loop. If all your team members know what matters most to your customers and they link that knowledge to their daily activities, the odds of keeping customers and obtaining new ones will increase. Yes, I know it sounds simple, even basic, but it takes some internal discipline.

Make it clear to your employees how their work fits in with other efforts and contributes to the end products you sell. It's not enough for Management, Sales, and

Marketing to know what your customers value most; *everyone* in the company must know. If *quality* is paramount, your raw materials buyer plays a critical role, perhaps just as critical as production or quality control. If *on-time delivery* is a top attribute, the shipping clerks and forklift drivers have a large impact. If *experience* or *technical expertise* or *industry certifications* are important, then HR must keep very accurate records to so Marketing and Sales can tout your specific competitive advantages. When *technical certifications* topped the list of attributes for one of our recent clients, they had to survey their own technicians to find out who had what certifications.

The farther your employees are from sales and marketing, the more often they must be reminded how they relate to meeting the company's strategic and financial goals. Hold them accountable and give them frequent reinforcement because without their best efforts, the goods or services you deliver, *and the way you deliver them*, which is usually the most critical need of your customers, will suffer. The credit card manufacturer did not make sure that the production manager knew of the urgency of the bank's order, and it cost them what was potentially millions in business. Volpi did spread the word internally, and is already reaping benefits.

When you keep your employees aware of how much impact their work has on meeting customers' needs, it gives them greater incentive to perform. It also provides them with a greater sense of pride, purpose, and meaning.

It is astounding how often organizations neglect this crucial step. Informed employees feel important and appreciated, which helps to create customers who feel satisfied and appreciated.

Informed employees are often sources of valuable information that you might not otherwise learn. Each and every employee has a unique vantage point and perspectives that others may not see. Often they can suggest changes that others might overlook. Ultimately, those changes could be substantial and play a significant role in your business's success. See our example of the wine kit manufacturer in Chapter Four.

CONNECTING THE DOTS

Many companies don't connect the dotted lines between what's most relevant to the customers, and the departments that deliver it. I have shown you the difference it makes, both ways. When you connect the dots it pays dividends; when you fail to, it's costly.

If you are in sales:

- Do you run into issues where you can't deliver what you promise? How have you communicated such breaches? Were they addressed?
- Which of your company's key performance indicators have you used successfully to address a customer's concern? What others might work also?
- Do you work in an organization where Sales might make recommendations or give management feedback on a routine basis?
- How can you ensure promises to customers are kept?

If you are in management:

- What feedback loop have you created for salespeople to communicate operational issues that cover customer concerns?
- Do you have an ongoing methodology for addressing such issues?
- How have communication gaps previously affected sales? What have you done about them?
- What have you done to ensure every department that affects a customer's priority is aware of their direct impact on that customer's satisfaction?

CHAPTER 8

Relevant Selling Relies on the Right Investments

ACCORDING TO MANAGEMENT GURU PETER DRUCKER, "Ninety percent of the information used in organizations is internally focused, and only ten percent is about the outside environment. This is exactly backwards."

Yes, it's vital for your company to run smoothly and efficiently. It's a given that you have to have quality products, knowledgeable personnel, and strong internal systems in place, but you also have to have the best, most reliable directional information. Like a pilot, every move you make should be based on having the correct bearings and following the right indicators. Pilots never guess which direction to fly; many companies do. If all your internal efforts are not based on solid information, your sales efforts will also be off course and they may not be relevant.

MIRROR, MIRROR, ON THE WALL...

Look from outside in. I often see companies that are wrapped up in themselves. Their self-images, who they think they are, and how they work often outweigh their customer focus. These companies tend to become obsessed with their culture. How they see and want to promote themselves – their brand identity – takes on exaggerated importance, while their customer focus wanes. All too often, their customers' wishes get lost in the shuffle. Sometimes, these businesses expect their customers to accept who they are and what they offer at face value, when the opposite should be true. Some cell phone companies come to mind – you know who they are.

It's not just companies that are afflicted with damaging narcissism. My friend Tom loved his cardiologist, a brilliant, personable surgeon who used the latest, state-of-the-art technology to perform the most difficult procedures and save lives. Whenever Tom made an office visit, the cardiologist spent the first ten minutes diagramming and explaining, in great detail, the intricacies of operations he recently performed. Although these stories were fascinating, they had nothing to do with Tom's treatment for his heart condition. And to make matters worse, the stories took up most of Tom's appointment time. During the last few minutes of the visits, the cardiologist finally focused on Tom. He asked Tom questions, responded to Tom's concerns, and gave advice – but he would do this at breakneck speed. Tom left each appointment feeling shortchanged; instead of being his cardiologist's prime focus, he felt like his audience. So he found a new cardiologist, one who gives him the time and attention he feels he deserves.

Some companies are in love with the fact that they're innovative, tech-savvy, and on the cutting edge. They pride themselves on being in the vanguard and at the head of the pack. I've seen manufacturers get so carried away with the notion of innovation that they make no attempt to learn what their customers actually want. Some dig themselves into holes "because we can." How many of you can use *all* the features on your cell phone? How many of you feel that you need all of them?

A promotion for Chuck Palahniuk's horror novel *Haunted* (Anchor, 2006) featured a quote from the book: "The difference between how you look and how you see yourself is enough to kill most people." Humorous by itself, I also think that it's pertinent to business. In my talks and presentations, I've adapted it to, "The difference between how you look and how you see yourself is enough to kill most *businesses.*"

Like individuals, businesses can have warped self-images. Just as people have spent fortunes on self-understanding and self-help, trying to find more realistic self-images as they journey through life, some of our clients have spent big dollars on branding, on fixing their culture, on renaming their companies. Yet businesses invest very little on learning how their customers truly perceive them.

UNNEEDED INNOVATION

Many companies have had misguided love affairs with innovation and technology. Now, don't get me wrong; innovation and technology are important and often essential. However, they must be *relevant*. Here are some examples of when they were not relevant:

Software. A company invested in building state-of-the-art software for on-line order tracking, only to subsequently learn that their customers ranked it at the very bottom of their buying criteria. What a waste! I'm sure the company was excited to have the newest and coolest technology, but their customers couldn't have cared less. It's wonderful to feel good about yourself and your business, but before you invest in the latest and greatest, find out what your customers will use.

Banking services. A large community bank was wiser and more fortunate. They were about to offer their customers free wealth management/brokerage services and expanded ATM locations. Since staffing for the new services and providing more ATMs was going to be quite costly, the bank decided check with their customers before implementing their plans. To the bank's surprise, they learned that neither the new services nor expanded ATM sites were highly regarded by either their retail or commercial customers. Most of their customers had long-standing relationships with wealth advisors, and research showed that the availability of wealth management service was not likely to make a difference in their banking choices. And since ATM's were everywhere, expanding their locations meant little to most customers. Consequently, the bank scrapped their plans and saved themselves a ton of money by not making irrelevant investments and trying to sell irrelevant services.

Printing. We were looking for a printer to deliver a pitch book for one of our clients on an extremely tight deadline. A number of bids came in, but Printer A stood out. They submitted an excellent proof and got the look, feel, and color of the book just right. Although Printer A quoted the highest price, they were the frontrunner because they had the best equipment, the latest technology, and turned out the highest-quality work. However, they didn't have the specialty paper needed to print the pitch book. They would have to order the paper, and as a result, the whole process, from getting the paper to delivering the book, would take thirteen days.

Printer B quoted a very similar price. Their work was of slightly lesser quality, but they had the specialty paper in stock. They guaranteed to deliver the pitch book to our client in five days. Since we were in a time squeeze, the decision was clear, Printer A – the paperless bidder – lost the job even though they probably would have done the best work. Turn-around time, the ability to quickly deliver what we wanted, not price or quality, was the clincher. Speed was the most relevant consideration; it was what our client wanted most. Although Printer A had the best equipment and technology, they lost the job because they had not made the right internal investments. If they had made the simple investment to stock the required paper, their sales force could have sold relevantly.

Hardware. Only two months after they introduced and heavily touted their TouchPad tablet PC, Hewlett-Packard (HP) announced that they would no longer sell that product.

When I heard this news, a couple of questions came to mind. Why did HP come out with the TouchPad to begin with? Did they feel they had to compete with Apple's market-dominating iPad? Or did they feel that they could capture a chunk of the iPad market? Did HP do their customer research? If so, did they actually listen to what customers were saying?

The voice of the customer should dictate your strategy, budget, and resource allocations, but it rarely does. Look to your customers for direction. Like the pilot's control panel, they should dictate your next moves. Discover what's most relevant to your customers by asking them.

On the other hand, look at the investments made by Amazon, a company built on technology. First, they revolutionized bookselling by promptly delivering books that customers ordered online. Then Amazon expanded their offerings to include a wide range of consumer goods.

Now, Amazon has made a number of investments that are focused on giving their customers what they want most: prompt delivery. They are growing their network of distribution centers to match increasing customer demand for faster shipping and a wider array of products. In 2011, Amazon added nine fulfillment centers and is prepared to build even more if demand increases. This comes on the heels Amazon's 2010 addition of thirteen fulfillment centers to its logistics network, and the launch of its Amazon Prime service that gives customers free two-day delivery for an annual membership fee. They continue to be the 8,000-pound gorilla because they know how to stay relevant.

OPERATIONALLY ALIGNED

In Chapter Two, I introduced you to CDC New England (CDC NE), which makes government secured SBA 504 loans to small businesses to finance the acquisition, expansion or modernization of fixed assets such as real estate or equipment. In 2009, CDC NE had about twenty competitors in their market, and ranked number five in sales. Since SBA 504 loans are generic, the products CDC NE offered were virtually identical to those of their competitors. So CDC NE called us in to help them differentiate themselves from the competition. As a result of our work together, the lender made major investments and strategic changes in their operation.

Kenneth J. Smith, the President and CEO of CDC NE's parent, BDC Capital, told me that we took the way they viewed themselves and turned it upside down. He said, "Your team showed us that how we viewed ourselves and how we defined our strengths and weaknesses was not as important as how the marketplace saw us. You convinced us that we had to go to our customers and measure how they perceived us. We needed to know what they thought we brought to the table and to find out what was most important to them." To be fair, we didn't show CDC NE the vulnerability in their viewpoint; we just showed them *how* to learn how their customers viewed them.

CDC NE commissioned a double-blind market survey of one hundred bank loan officers throughout New

England. Specifically, CDC NE wanted to know what the loan officers wanted most and the criteria they used in referring loans to one company rather than others.

Step one was to survey loan officers and learn why they made their referral decisions. Prior to the survey, management didn't know exactly what the loan officers wanted most. Management believed that they referred business because of CDC NE's *prudence in making good loans*. As I wrote in Chapter Two, they also thought that most of their business was based on their *good-ol' boy network* – their relationships with the loan officers.

CDC NE's survey found that loan officers didn't rank *prudence* or *relationships* at the top their lists. Instead, their top priorities were *speed of response, problem solving,* and *communication and accessibility,* which CDC NE's management had not considered.

By far, the loan officers' top priority was *speed*. They wanted quick answers. While CDC NE still needed to be prudent and make good loans, they had to do so quickly. And while loans were being processed, they had to keep the bankers in the loop.

The customer data gave CDC NE a great foundation on which to build. It broke down the main reasons for the loan officers' referral decisions and gave the lender specific targets to meet.

We met with CDC NE's senior management team to review the survey results, set goals, and develop strategies. We discussed what the bank loan officers said they wanted most and explored how CDC NE could excel in delivering on their top priorities.

"Since *speed* was of such great importance to our referral sources," Smith said, "we broke down every segment of our loan processing operation, analyzed it, and examined how we could make it faster. If a process took two days, we looked at how we could cut that time in half and then cut it again. We examined every step, every process and procedure, because if we were going to market our rapid response, we had to be sure that we could consistently deliver it. We looked at all our processes, personnel assignments, allocations, and tasks, and redesigned them to speed up our processes. To keep on track, we continued to hold these internal operations meetings every two weeks."

CDC NE made new hires. They recruited people who had been top performers with other organizations and would not be satisfied working for a fifth place concern. The lender looked for people who understood the importance of knowing what customers wanted most and would make sure to give it to them. CDC NE hired recruits who took pride in the company's progress, and knew that the company's major goals were to grow the business and create an organization that would compete to be number one in their market.

CDC NE then created systems to coordinate and measure their internal improvements. Every loan transaction involves two customers, a loan officer and a borrower. Several specialists at CDC NE are involved in processing each loan: a business development officer who sources the transaction and sends it internally; an underwriter who secures the financing; and a closer who prepares the closing documents and gets them processed and signed. To make each transaction run smoothly and on track, CDC NE created a new customer service concierge to oversee and coordinate all communications.

Now one person, the concierge, supervises each transaction. Every customer is given her name and phone number. She fields all questions and regularly checks in with bankers, loan officers, borrowers, and in-house staff members to make sure that everything is in place and that the loan is moving on course. The concierge also provides updates and status reports and asks about questions and needs.

Loan officers and borrowers are given the concierge's company cell phone number and she is expected to answer 24/7. She is accessible to customers at all times and for anything they might need.

When each loan closes, CDC NE sends the loan officer and the borrower a questionnaire that asks him or her to rate the lender's performance. The first five questions are about the top five attributes from the market research. The sixth and last question asks if the loan officer or borrower would recommend CDC NE. A $25 gift certificate from Dunkin' Donuts is enclosed with the questionnaire as a way to thank them for answering their questions. The concierge is in charge of sending the customer service questionnaires, and recording and compiling the responses. The data compiled gives CDC NE information that they use to continually measure, analyze, and enhance their loan processing. The concierge also posts all the responses in the company lunchroom for all employees to see. "The results have been great," said Ken.

Note the benefits to CDC NE and to their customers:

- The questionnaire is quick and easy – six questions on a half page, with a 1 – 5 rating scale.
- Accurate – only the top five tested attributes are discussed.
- CEO Ken Smith's cell phone is on the questionnaire, so if the loan officer has any significant issues, or even just a question, he or she can call Ken directly.
- Easy data to compile, providing the proof for new competitive advantage statements.
- Easy for the business development managers to use in face-to-face meetings with loan officers.

The end result is a win-win-win for CDC NE, the loan officers, and the borrowers!

CDC NE also designed a deal-tracker log to monitor every stage of the lending process. The amount of time that each stage takes is recorded and that information is used to make each stage more efficient and faster. Standards for each stage were also set so the company's personnel know what they are expected to achieve and in what period of time. Every two weeks, each of those pieces are measured and reviewed. In that way, CDC NE knows the turn around time on each stage.

Employees' compensation is tied to how well they perform. They are paid at a base level and also receive a variable amount of compensation tied to the number of transactions they process and the speed with which they process them. The incentive is clear. From the get-go, CDC NE's employees know that speed is crucial and that they will be evaluated and compensated for quickly processing deals.

Knowing what customers want is just one part of the equation. Essential information must be communicated to prospects and customers to convince them to give you business. They must be convinced that your company can give them what they want most.

When CDC NE is being considered as a lender, they let loan officers and borrowers know that they are dedicated to delivering what the customer wants most. They demonstrate that CDC NE is the best company to fulfill their top requirements – speed, problem solving, communications and accessibility – with data history that proves it.

To make sure that the message got out powerfully, clearly, and relevantly, we helped CDC NE develop competitive advantage statements that show customers the reasons they should do business with the firm. For example, a statement may say, "99% of CDC New England loans are qualified within 24 hours." This statement is factual and measurable and can be supplemented by marketing materials that explain why.

CDC NE has also totally revamped their website to show that they excel in the areas their customers want most. The company turned a static website, which had the feel of a brochure, into a more viral and interactive site. When you visit the site, you see all sorts of facts about their speed of response, problem solving, communication, and accessibility. The site also provides a number of examples that show loan officers and borrowers how CDC NE quickly solved many of the problems they might face, and got their customers the money they needed.

The home page of CDC NE's website asks, "WHY CHOOSE CDC NEW ENGLAND?" Then it answers the question:

Fastest Loan Approvals
- 99% of CDC New England loans are qualified within 24 hours.

Creative Problem Solving
- Check your loan status online for real-time application updates.

Simple Application Process
- 98% of customers rate their experience with CDC New England as "Excellent."

After each item, visitors can click on a "Read case studies" link.

All of CDC NE's messaging materials have been revamped. Email blasts are sent to emphasize how quickly the lender processes loans. The company's sales approach was also tightened. Instead of giving vague and generalized reasons why loan officers and borrowers should do business with CDC NE, salespeople are now specific. They focus on delivering the most relevant sales messages by stressing that the company qualifies loans in twenty-four hours (the fastest in the industry). They also stress that CDC NE makes good loans; they inform customers that the SBA measures failure and delinquency rates, and CDC NE has among the best results in the industry.

In the face of a dismal financial market, CDC NE's business has soared. Since they have plugged into the voices of their customers, their revenues and profits have grown dramatically. In just over a year, the number of transactions closed annually jumped from twenty-five to sixty, and as of this writing they are on track to close more than eighty transactions by the end of their fiscal year.

In terms of market share, CDC NE has moved from fifth to second in New England. When they were fifth in size, the top provider was five times their size. Now, CDC NE is within striking distance of the leader and they plan to become the largest soon by opening new offices and adding new people.

"Now, when bankers need something fast, we get more calls," Ken Smith summarized. "We're a work in progress, but we're getting there."

WOOD ON YOUR TIME

One-size-fits-all policies rarely work, as Intermountain Wood Products (IWP) discovered. Since 1931, IWP has supplied a wide selection of hardwood and related products to the cabinet, casework, and millwork industries. It also sells an assortment of prefinished and unfinished flooring and accessories, such as finishes, tools, sand paper, and glue. Based in Salt Lake City, Utah, the company has ten distribution centers in Colorado, Idaho, Montana, Nebraska, Utah and Washington, from which they sell their products. Each center has its own warehouse, trucks, drivers, and a sales staff. All together, IWP has a fleet of forty-two trucks. Approximately sixty percent of all IWP sales are "will call" at one of their ten distribution centers. The remaining forty percent, IWP delivers to customers.

IWP was hit hard when the recession crippled the construction and building industries. To get what business was left, their competitors cut their prices. Like so many businesses, IWP felt forced to compete on price and accept reduced margins. So they wanted to find better alternatives.

Before I describe our work with IWP, let me tell

you about this unique company. The corporate culture centers on love and appreciation of the outdoors, nature, and the environment. IWP is a steward for the environment that is committed to "the longevity of this planet and those who live on it." Company retreats always involve outdoor activities, and when we met the executive team, it was at a hotel at the entrance to magnificent Zion National Park. The day after our meeting, executive team members hiked the advanced trails at the park.

Company president Ben Banks is a devoted bicyclist. Each summer, he and his son ride back roads from state to state, and the following summer, they start where they left off. The ride started in Astoria, Oregon. So far they've gotten to Springfield, Missouri, and their ultimate destination is Yorktown, Virginia. In the process, Ben has seen much of America in ways most people don't. He has gained unique first-hand knowledge, insights, and understandings about our forests, resources, and wood, the raw products that IWP sells.

We started our engagement by asking IWP's management team what they thought prospects and customers wanted most. When we aggregated their guesses, the highest vote getter was *product consistency,* which got six votes out of sixteen voters. When compared with responses from prospects and customers, those six voters turned out to be correct – it was number one.

However, when it came to *on-time delivery,* there was a substantial difference. Overall, IWP's staff placed it eighth, and no one ranked it first. In contrast, the prospects and customers surveyed rated *on-time delivery* as the second most important attribute.

Learning how relevant *on-time delivery* was to their prospects and customers was the first step. Management immediately recognized the importance of that information because although just forty percent of IWP's sales require deliveries, eighty-five percent of the company's overall revenue comes from delivered materials. Next, management had to find out what *on-time delivery* actually meant to customers. What was acceptable as *on time*? Were customers ordering two weeks in advance to make sure that their shipments were on hand when needed? Or, did they need to receive deliveries on a specific date and time, say by 4:00 PM on Thursday? If so, were they placing orders in the morning and expecting to receive them by 4:00 PM? Was there any leeway on their deadlines?

To answer these questions, management instructed branch managers to ask each customer what *on-time delivery* meant to them. When all the answers were compiled, IWP got a collection of replies that were all over the place. Nearly every customer defined *on time* differently. We've experienced this same conundrum with many clients. Yet most businesses continue to define *on-time delivery* with a broad brush, and usually from their own perspective. Therefore, they're not always relevant.

Not so with IWP. The company issued a corporate edict. On *each order*, IWP's sales force was to ask the customer what *on-time delivery* meant, and whatever the answer, they were to meet it.

Below are the opening paragraphs of the memo that the company sent to their Distribution Center (DC) managers:

ON-TIME DELIVERY

Our standard for on-time delivery will be essentially whatever the customer wants. In other words, we will let the customer define what *on time* is. If it is a particular day, or a specific time of day, or a general am or pm, it really doesn't matter as long as it has been communicated to the customer. Some DC's have gone out of their way to *not* make commitments if possible on deliveries. This is not the way to build excellent and enviable customer service.

The Management Group cannot see a way to develop a one-size-fits-all definition to this measurement. Whatever the customer expects and whatever we commit to, will be the definition. Once we have communicated to the customer when an order will be delivered and they have agreed, that will be the time or standard to which we will hold ourselves accountable. However, we will all measure and track our performance the same way.

Then the memo set forth instructions that IWP's distribution centers were to follow in order to implement the new on-time-delivery policy.

Ben Banks, IWP's president says, "In this environment, anything you can do that appears to be playing offense, as opposed to playing defense, is a plus, because during tough times we get hunkered down into playing defense to survive. It's hard to convince your people that there are offensive plays if they just look for them. In fact, we engaged Smart Advantage to bring us their competitive advantage process as just such an offensive play. This process brought people together and forced them to look at our business and it has given them a sense of enthusiasm about the business, if not the actual market conditions. If nothing else, it's saved us mentally and emotionally during this really, really ugly time, and has positioned us as we come out of it to be far better than when we went into it. And I think our people are seeing that because when I read their reports, they seem to be hungry for applications of the strategies we've learned. So there's been no push back at all. In fact, just the opposite, they were anxious to participate in the process and anxious to implement it."

In our work, we frequently see companies overrate the importance of respect, reputation, and their history. In their messaging, they emphasize how long they have been in business and/or that they are a family run business that builds relationships.

We gently remind our clients that customers care about one thing: WIIFM, or "What's in it for me?" Let's be honest: the fact that your business is old and reputable may also mean that it is ancient and fossilized. Your venerable history may be of no advantage or utility to your customers. They only want to know what you can do for them today. No one will buy a Chrysler just because the company has been in business since 1925 – the company has to earn new customers every year. Like a pop music star, you're only as good as your last hit record. Our research has shown that prospects and customers aren't typically swayed by longevity. It's not at the top of their buying criteria. When a business was founded and by whom may be interesting, even fascinating, but what you can do today is what really counts.

In fact, many of today's customers prefer to deal with young, upstart companies. They assume such companies are innovative, hungry, and on the cutting edge. They think that they can offer more with less baggage. Many equate "old and established" with "bureaucratic and out-of-date," and they don't want to pay a premium for a company's past. So be careful if this is a cornerstone of your marketing. Ask your customers if your history is relevant.

IWP fell into this trap. Management thought that the fourth most important item to prospects and buyers was *recognition in the industry* for being a provider that was honest, reliable, and financially stable. However, customers and prospects listed it as only thirteenth in importance to them.

Although IWP had a long standing, good reputation,

their messages were not conveying the solid value that they clearly were providing *right now*. They needed to make their prospects and customers confident that it was worth paying a slightly higher price to buy from IWP. We asked IWP's management, "If eighty-two percent of prospects consider you the best, why are you competing on price?" The answer seemed to be that IWP assumed that many of their buyers think that "wood is wood," so they buy on price. Unlike many of our clients who can't wait to tout the features of their product (even though they may be selling a commodity), IWP realized that they actually were selling a commodity, but they failed to capitalize on all their other differentiators.

As I mentioned before, I always tell my clients that what the customer wants from you is not so much "what" you sell, but rather "how" you deliver what you sell. The reason is that most goods and services can become commodities that someone can usually sell for less. Caving in on price is easy, but costly. When companies fail to sell what is relevant, in this case *consistent products* and *on-time delivery*, then price will, by default, be the tiebreaker.

BLIND SPOTS

Like all of us, most businesses can have blind spots. Although they may be experts in their fields, they may not realize the importance of things that buyers rate highly. Straub's Fine Grocers, like nearly all the companies we studied, had their share of blind spots.

Since 1901, when they delivered groceries by horse and buggy, Straub's has been operating in St. Louis, Missouri. Long before Wal-Mart had greeters, even before Sam Walton had stores, founder William A. Straub stood at his store's front door and personally welcomed each customer. He established the warm, friendly tradition that remains the hallmark of Straub's to this day.

Personal service, and better and unusual products, have continuously been Straub's forte. Besides offering top quality goods and service, they go to great lengths to fill their customers' requests, including those for rare, exotic items that they come across during their travels. When customers wanted chocolate-coated grasshoppers and ants, Straub's provided them.

The company now has four fine food markets in the area, and an internet outlet. Each store features gourmet grocery products, the best national brand items, and an award-winning, full service meat department. Each store also offers made-to-order deli, high-end seafood, the freshest produce, and barbecue freshly smoked onsite. The best chicken salad in North America! My only regret is that Straub's doesn't have a store in my neighborhood.

Trust me, strolling through Straub's fabulous stores is a major sensory treat. As I moved from department to department, I was greeted by one delicious scent after another and a continuum of glorious sights. Six different soups made in the store, lots of free samples, and thirty-five brands of root beer! What a treat! It was sensory overload and I enjoyed every second. And the best way I can describe the employees is "friendly pride." They are positively eager to show you the pleasures of their store. I swear these folks could teach a thing or two to Disney's tour guides, and that's going some!

When we polled Straub's staff to find out what they thought customers wanted most, we received 117 responses from virtually the entire staff, which is extremely unusual. Typically, we get fewer team members who vote, and they are primarily executives, department heads, and some salespeople. True to their culture, CEO Trip Straub asked every employee to vote.

The majority of Straub's staff thought that *welcoming customers to stores* was most important to prospects and customers. After all, that's the Wal-Mart greeter philosophy that now is a staple in many retail businesses. At Straub's, everyone greets each customer, tries hard to remember each customer's name, and makes special efforts to offer individual help. This is all done with a sincere, warm, "Midwest" approach, not a hard-sell tactic.

When the results of Straub's survey were tallied, *freshness of food* topped the list. Second was *food safety*. Ironically, when we were designing the customer research survey, I suggested including *food safety* as an attribute to test, but Straub's management was reluctant because they felt *food safety* was a given. Fortunately, we convinced them it was worth testing because we learned that the respondents were clear about its importance. And Straub's is glad we included it in the survey.

In another twist of fate, Straub's may have benefited from one of their competitor's advertising campaign. We were told that the competitor had conducted annual research and then made *food safety* the centerpiece of their campaign, which heightened the public's awareness of the importance of food safety. Although Straub's was second to none in that area, they never talked about food safety in their sales or marketing messages. Now, however, Straub's could capitalize on the increased public awareness and tout their outstanding food safety record.

Besides refocusing their messages, Straub's went even further. They invested in even higher company-wide food safety standards. In addition, Straub's increased their intensive, company-wide food safety training programs. Now, all their employees must undergo refresher training and are held accountable for maintaining Straub's high standards. As I write, Straub's food safety measures not only meet, but now exceed all governmental requirements.

The third attribute most valued by their shoppers was a good *produce department* followed in fourth place by *welcoming customers to stores*. Straub's knew the importance of both of these items, but didn't know how to communicate its excellence in these areas. Straub's sells only the finest freshest produce; even items grown in California were off the tree or vine and on Straub's shelves within twenty-four hours. Every day, the company squeezed oranges at their stores to provide the freshest juice, but their containers didn't indicate the date when the juice was squeezed. Now the dates are printed on Straub's orange juice containers so customers know their freshness and safety levels. No chance of spoiling – freshly squeezed every few hours!

While Straub's was learning where to shift their focus, there was another surprising twist. Just as the company was about to invest heavily to improve their online ordering process, they got the survey results: shoppers placed *online ordering* near the bottom of their lists. When we showed management that result, Trip Straub said, "Well, that just saved me a lot of money." We all had a good chuckle and the entire staff realized that they saved some valuable resources by *not* investing in what was not relevant to their customers.

Perhaps for their customers, the delightful experience of shopping at a Straub's store makes the idea of ordering online pointless. This demonstrates that unlike at Amazon, where the book you order online is the exact same book you can find on the bookshelf, the products offered by Straub's beg to be seen and smelled and inspected by their discerning customers.

MEASURE, THEN BRAG

Bouchard Insurance is a privately held insurance agency, founded in 1948. They are headquartered in Clearwater and have offices up and down the Gulf Coast of Florida.

They are currently headed by the bright young executive Doug Bishop. Doug is only the third CEO of Bouchard since the agency was founded, which speaks volumes about Bouchard's stability.

Bouchard specializes in providing insurance for large companies. They handle all kinds of insurance, but their main business is employee benefit and workers' compensation insurance. They contacted us to explore ways that they might ensure their relevance and expand their revenues.

"The customer research that we commissioned had a few surprises," Mr. Bishop explains. "We spent a lot of time and money building strong *loss control resources* in our organization, which was important, but when our clients prioritized what was most important to them, *reputation for good loss control* systems was number four with workers' compensation purchasers.

"*Quick response time* was most important – the fact that someone would get back to our clients quickly. Although we did a good job of responding quickly, we didn't do a good job of measuring how quickly we respond and then touting that. So we began measuring our response time so that we can tell prospects and clients."

"You can say that you do certain things very well," Bishop states, "but if it's not something that is important to the client or prospect then you're wasting your resources. When we got the survey results back, we examined how those results matched with our competitive advantages. Then, we took a close look at the top four or five items that were most important to our clients and built strong value statements around them."

Bouchard is still going through the measurement process and wants to wait for at least a year before quantifying the specific benefits that it received. However, one result was apparent quickly: the increase in the sales force's level of energy. And an energized sales force invariably generates more sales.

"Our sales force is always looking for ways to make themselves stand out in comparison to their competition. They're eager to create opportunities," Bishop said. "Now, we've given them tools that they've gobbled up. The competitive advantage statements that we developed have become mantras around the office. They're in our marketing materials and have given us something that is going to give our sales force energy and confidence, which should produce more sales."

We get our clients to focus just as much on resource allocation as on messaging, because relevant selling depends on relevant resource allocation. Investing resources, both human and financial, in things *not* relevant to your customers, is wasteful. We then make sure they are measuring that which matters, and if they are not, we drive them to begin those measurements.

Sometimes, less is more, and simplification is the best innovation. Before making an investment, ask if it will help you deliver what your customers want. Strategic planners typically ask CEOs and/or management teams,

"What's your vision and mission?" They also frequently say, "Where do you want to be in one year, two years, and down the road?"

In my opinion, the better question is, "What do your customers want this year, next year, and beyond?"

Again, look from the outside in. Learn what your customers want and give it to them. Think relevance, relevance, relevance. If you do, both you and your customers will get what you want, and your profits will soar.

RELEVANT INVESTMENTS

Make sure company's business planning and investments reflect your customers' most desired deliverables. Don't be mesmerized by non-essentials. Explore the following questions with your team:

- Are we too focused on our commodity/product/service rather than how we get it to our customers?
- Can we provide what customers or prospects want, when they want it?
- Will buyers find our investments and strategies relevant and in alignment with what they want? Will our investments and strategies help us deliver what our customers value most? For example, if they want a live person in the U.S. on the phone, do we staff a call center around the clock? Do we offer live chat? If not, then we are not relevant. (Hint: see figure 5-A.)
- Do our customers really care that we excel in areas that are not important to them? For example, if we have extra salespeople to provide post-sale support, but only a few customers use it or want it, then we are not selling relevance. Or, if we offer online billing, but no one uses it, then why are we touting it in sales calls?
- Should we implement strategic objectives to add five new bells and whistles to our product when our customers only care only about the one our product already had?

CHAPTER 9

Finding Relevance
Is Easier Than You Think

T HERE IS A MYTH KNOWN SIMPLY AS THE GORDIAN Knot. At one time, about 1,000 B.C., the Phrygians of ancient Turkey were without a king. An oracle decreed that the next man to enter the city driving an ox-cart should become their king. A peasant farmer named Gordias drove into town on an ox-cart, and the priests declared him king. The treasured ox-cart was tied to a post with an intricate knot – as it turned out, another oracle had prophesied that the one to untie the knot would become the king of all Asia.

Centuries passed and no one could untie the knot.

Seven hundred years later, when Alexander the Great

arrived, the ox-cart still stood in the palace at Gordium. Alexander attempted to untie the knot. When he could not find the end to the knot to unbind it, he simply sliced it in half with a stroke of his sword, producing the required ends.

Many companies think that actually knowing what their customers and prospects want most is not possible. So they guess (see Chapter Three). Since they're guessing, their guesses differ (see Chapter Four). Sometimes they guess wrong (ninety percent of the time!). And the results can be disastrous (HPs TouchPad, Apple's Newton, New Coke). But it doesn't have to be this way. There is a fairly simple solution to this seemingly intractable problem: a sword stroke that will cut the Gordian knot.

Pros and cons exist in most decisions we make, including how we obtain the voice of our customers and learn what they really value. This chapter will focus on free and inexpensive methods of finding what customers want, and describe the benefits and tradeoffs of each. Chapter Ten will discuss how to purchase the kind of double-blind customer market research I've described throughout the book.

INDUSTRY ASSOCIATIONS

Industry associations can be a good source of general market research. Your trade association may already have research studies on hand that could be of enormous benefit to you. So check to see what research it has conducted recently.

You can also ask your industry association to conduct research for you. After all, they may need a place to spend all the dues you've paid over the years. Some associations will commission a study and then split the expense with you. That's what Clarity Products did (see below). They may also divide the cost among a group of members or even pay for the study from their coffers. Some of our clients have done this with their associations.

The upside of partnering with an association on research projects is that it can be considerably cheaper than if you have to pick up the entire tab. If the association spreads the cost between its members, your costs will probably be minimal. Studies sponsored by a trade association may also be more extensive because the association may be able to afford to spend more than you can for comprehensive research.

Partnering on research with an association can increase your profile in your industry. The mere fact that you partner with an association will help position you as an authority and a well-connected force in the industry. If you become the voice of the study – the person who explains or introduces it to members, the public, and the press – you may receive some publicity when and after the study is released. You can capitalize on your relationship by holding press conferences and events when the study is released. On these ventures, you can partner with the association, with other parties, or go it alone.

The downsides of working with an industry association are (1) the results are usually made available to all association members – who may be your competitors; (2) the results are typically general in nature; and (3) you will not be able to separate your customers' responses from your prospects' responses. When an association commissions research, it also may not focus on the issues and attributes that are most important to your specific customers. And you may not get competitive intelligence that ranks you in comparison to your top competitors.

CHOOSE A LIKE MINDED PARTNER

Find partners that will match up well with you. Clarity Products, a maker of telephones and other communications devices for the hard of hearing, was interested in conducting research on a telephone designed for arthritis sufferers, so it partnered on a study with the Arthritis Foundation. The Arthritis Foundation's sponsorship gave the study greater stature and gave the results more clout. People didn't question its results as they might have had Clarity proceeded on its own.

Find the right partner by determining who could use the same information you need. Consider partnering with your industry peers. Peers who don't compete with you in your geographic market can be ideal partners and joining with them will cut your costs. When you partner with them, it could also pave the way for other joint ventures.

Auto dealerships pioneered the formation of industry peer groups. Dealers joined with other dealers, who didn't compete on the same turf, to share statistics and best practices. They also acted as a board of advisors for each other. Other industries have followed suit.

A friend of mine named Don Campion is CEO of Banyan Air Service, a Fixed-Base Operator (FBO) in Fort Lauderdale known for servicing private jets. He belongs to a "Group of 20" FBOs that meet once a month to share data and which has cooperatively purchased research.

Peer groups now exist in more and more industries including construction, health care, and manufacturing, to name just a few. Does your industry have such a group, or could you form one, that would afford you the opportunity to share the cost of market research?

Find partnership candidates at meetings and conferences. At these events, members compare metrics, discuss trends, and help each other on matters of common interest. Often, they pool resources to conduct research studies. Although many of those in attendance will be in your industry, they may not compete in the same geographic areas or provide the same goods or services. Ask other attendees if they're interested, or can suggest potential partners.

Other possible partnership candidates could be businesses in your industry that operate at different levels or sell to different markets. For example, if you're a manufacturer, you could hook up with a sales and marketing firm, an advertising group, distributors, wholesalers, or suppliers.

INTERNS: PRO'S AND CON'S

Hire an intern to handle your research study. Many business schools will let you post a notice at their placement office. Or you can go directly to a dean, professor, counselor, or advisor to help you find students who have some experience in designing and analyzing customer market research. Usually, faculty or staff members know the best candidates and can refer several qualified students.

The upside to using an intern – Hiring interns is less expensive than hiring a professional firm. If the intern receives course credit for working with you, all the better because he or she will work hard and you may not have to pay him or her. Plus, you may find a good candidate for permanent employment with your firm.

The downside – Most surveys require at least seventy to one hundred completed interviews to provide statistically significant "actionable" data. This might require you to make between 1,000 and 6,000 attempts. So conducting your survey may not be the right job for everyone. Conducting customer research surveys takes diligence, hard work, and someone with the constitution of a bulldog. In online surveys, the amount of data received can be overwhelming and it may take an intern a great deal of time to tabulate. Surveying is hard, time-consuming work. Not everyone can do it well.

More downsides (as if you wanted more!) –

(1) Interns may become disinterested, do a half-hearted job, or poop out and quit. As they work, they may decide that this is not the field for them or they can get bored. Either way, they can walk and leave you in the lurch.

(2) Since interns aren't professional researchers, they will be learning on the job. Some may catch on quickly, but others may have long learning curves that prolong the project. They may ask a million questions that can divert your staff's time. Also, their inexperience can initially make them prone to errors and mistakes.

(3) If your intern actually interviews respondents, your study will not be double blind because the interviewer will know that your company has commissioned the project. Such knowledge could affect the validity and veracity of the interviews. Little things like wording, pauses, tone of voice, and inflections could unintentionally convey opinions and/or bias.

Sarah Needleman, who produces Wall Street Journal's *In Charge* publication for small businesses, wrote this about using help from schools:

> ""Entrepreneurs should use caution when approaching a college or university for support," says Howard Anderson, a senior lecturer on entrepreneurship at the MIT Sloan School of Management in Cambridge, Mass. "The advice of a college student is not quite the same as advice from someone with several years of industry experience," he says. "For the student, this is a learning experience."
>
> "Also keep in mind that schools are typically willing to go only so far in helping entrepreneurs," Mr. Anderson says. "While it's reasonable to request tips for tackling a specific problem or assistance with a project, for example, asking students to do administrative work or help build a business from scratch is not." ("Go Back to School for Free Help," *Wall Street Journal*, September 25, 2011)

ONLINE SURVEYS

A cheaper, but not easier, option is to conduct an online survey. Online surveys can provide valuable information less expensively than other data collection methods. One potential risk with online surveys is that they may not be double-blind; the respondents will know you are sponsoring the research if you send an email blast from your company's web address or you post the online survey on your website. Internet surveys can be good when you want a fairly large and geographically diverse sample. If they're conducted via email, you can get quick results once the questions are emailed. On the other hand, the time involved for set up, advance letters or emails, follow-ups, administration, and analysis can be extensive. As an alternative to lists, you can advertise the survey. However, that alternative can be slower, less efficient, and can create validity concerns because the respondents are self-selected. Online surveys are not appropriate for every research project. Not everyone has internet access, which limits the respondent pool, and many people will not participate in online surveys. Studies have found that the demographic that responds to online questionnaire invitations is generally biased to younger people (*Questionnaire Methodology*, John Wiley & Sons, Inc., 2004).

As I said, online surveys can be less expensive than other research data gathering approaches, but not easier. They may not be easier for two reasons:

First, a good questionnaire must ask precisely what you want to know. So it's hard to craft. All questions must be clear, unambiguous, and relevant. They cannot contain extraneous information. If they do, they can frustrate respondents and they may not give you the information you need. Drafting precise questions is part science and part art. The art part takes expertise.

The importance of well-written survey questions recently made headlines. After Bank of America set off a firestorm by announcing that they were going to charge customers a $5 monthly debit card usage fee on purchases in September of 2011, the Credit Union National Association (CUNA) reported a surge in credit union membership. According CUNA, their survey found that 650,000 new members joined credit unions after B of A's announcement in November, 2011. During that time, the Association claimed, credit unions added $4.5 billion in savings.

About a month later, a red-faced CUNA admitted that the numbers it reported were too high. Instead of gaining 650,000 new accounts and $4.5 billion in new deposits, it said that only 214,000 new members signed up – two-thirds less than first reported. And deposits actually *dipped* by $400 million.

"We were not precise enough in drafting the questionnaire," the Association's chief economist told *The American Banker* publication. The survey questions may have confused those surveyed and caused them to combine the figures they provided for "new accounts" with those they gave for "new members."

The second reason online surveys are not easier: even if an online questionnaire is well written, you may not reach the right respondents. For example, you may want your health care survey to be answered by surgeons, but the individual respondents may be the surgeon's nurse, nurse practitioner, receptionist, or even a teenage daughter who has access to the survey, but no knowledge of her mother's surgical practice. Some techniques for avoiding this pitfall include calling first, giving them a time-limited password, and using several cross-tabbed screening questions. However, each of these techniques adds complexity (read: cost) to your survey, and requires expertise to craft correctly.

Let me tell you about four popular online survey support sites that offer a free version: Survey Monkey, SurveyTool, Polldaddy, and Zoomerang. Each of these survey companies offers on its website a free version of its product plus subscription plans that let you conduct surveys frequently. The free versions include basic survey features and all are user friendly. It takes about thirty minutes to set up a quick survey. Then you send the survey as an email blast to your customers or paste it onto your website. Some online survey companies may provide discounts for nonprofit organizations. Before you sign up, check on the plans and their features because they change from time to time.

Survey Monkey (www.surveymonkey.com),
Basic Service – Free
10-question limit
100 responses

Create survey questions from 31 templates and
15 question types
Support: video tutorials

Besides the free Basic Plan, Survey Monkey offers
Select, Gold and Platinum Plans at varying costs. For a
professional user, the Platinum Plan can be well worth
the price because it lets you run an unlimited number
of surveys and get an unlimited number of responses. It
also gives you better data format/table analysis. Some of
our clients with employees spread over a wide geography
use Survey Monkey to do internal surveys – interest in
daycare, plans for continuing education, even voting on
attributes.

Survey Tool (www.surveytool.com),
Free Service
Three surveys per month
Unlimited questions per survey
20 responses per survey
50 email addresses per survey
Over 35 pre-written, fully customizable templates
18 different question types
Surveys can go out on Facebook, Twitter, or any
popular media sharing website.

Three subscription plans are also offered: Basic, Pro,
and Enterprise. The most comprehensive and expensive, the Enterprise Plan, gets you a dedicated account

manager, multiple unlimited user accounts, unlimited surveys, unlimited responses, and unlimited email invites per survey. You also get free monthly sample credits and priority telephone support.

Polldaddy (www.polldaddy.com)
Free Service
10 questions per survey
200 responses per month
50 email addresses per survey
Basic reports for polls, surveys, and quizzes
Surveys responses can be collected from iPad or iPhone

Polldaddy comes from the same company as Wordpress, the largest self-hosted blogging tool in the world. If you use Wordpress, Polldaddy might seem more "intuitive" to you. Two subscription plans are also offered: Professional, at $200 per year, and Corporate, at $899 per year (at press time). The Corporate account gets you unlimited responses per month, unlimited questions per survey, the content does not contain Polldaddy links (the free version does), ten user accounts, custom domain mapping, and a number of other features.

Zoomerang (www.zoomerang.com)
Basic Service – Free
Unlimited surveys and polls
12 questions

Design questions from scratch or from six basic templates
100 responses

You can create surveys from scratch or from templates. A large variety are available that are specific to industries.

Support: Email support. Phone support costs $25 per call. Live training online, tutorials, demos, quick start guides, and resource center.

Two additional plans, Pro and Premium, are also offered. Each offers over 100 templates, unlimited questions, and unlimited responses.

Some online surveys, usually the free versions, will delete your data after ten days. Some allow you to copy or download it, some don't.

WARNING! It isn't easy to write unambiguous questions and put them in the right order. It's hard to select the right ranges for a multiple-choice question and to know when an open-ended question is best. Having one of your employees handle online surveys can be dangerous, because unless he or she is experienced with survey forms and techniques, he or she may not structure the questions well. It's best to have an experienced market research consultant construct your survey. Then, if you want to conduct subsequent surveys, you can use in-house employees who worked with the consultant if they learned enough to run them well.

Debby Schlesinger-Hellman, PRC, executive vice

president of the marketing research firm Schlesinger Associates, points out that, "The length of a survey is very important. If it takes more than fifteen to twenty minutes, it's tough online. Surveys that long are also tough on the phone, but on the phone you're hearing their voice and you can tell whether they've lost interest and you may know what you have to do to keep them going. On line, you don't have that option. Ten minutes is probably the sweet spot for an online survey, twelve minutes for telephone surveys. For longer surveys, you have to pay them and it really becomes not just a survey, but an interview."

MEASURING SURVEY RELIABILITY

I'm frequently asked, "How many people must be surveyed to get accurate results?" No hard line exists and the answer usually depends on two basic statistical concepts:

1. **Range of error.** When survey results are reported, they are usually accompanied by an error rate: a certain plus or minus percentage, for example, plus or minus ten percent. That means that the results are not off by more than ten percent and that the survey findings are likely to be replicated if you went out to a much larger sample size (within plus or minus ten percent).
2. **Confidence level.** This figure reflects the degree of

confidence in the survey results. Confidence level is also expressed as a percentage. It is the same as saying if you were to conduct the survey multiple times, how often you would expect to get similar results (within the range of error.) When the confidence level is ninety percent, the researcher would anticipate getting the same results nine out of ten times.

Both concepts, range of error and confidence level, work together to describe a survey's accuracy. If a survey has an error rate of five percent and a confidence level of ninety percent and the survey is conducted 100 times or 1,000 times, the findings should be within ±five percent of the result of the first survey (in nine out of ten cases).

Some industries require high accuracy level percentages. Nuclear engineers doing probabilistic risk analysis have high standards. They usually insist on at least a "95-95" standard for their statistically based decisions. That means their results must be ninety-five percent accurate ninety-five percent of the time. Political pollsters aim for 3-4 percent error rate. When we mere mortals conduct telephone interviews that do not involve radioactivity or politics, a "90%-90%" ratio can be reasonable.

COMPETITIVE INTELLIGENCE

It is not unusual for companies to be surprised by their competition. Clients frequently tell me that the only time they get essential information about a competitor is when it steals an important customer or employee. They sound like deserted spouses after their partners left. They look at you blankly and mutter, "I had no idea anything was wrong."

The key to effective competitive intelligence is getting information early on so you know what your competitors are doing and can predict what they will do next. One of our recent clients told us about their technique for finding out how the competition took customers from them. They referred to the process as "customer exit interviews."

We asked, "Why on earth are you waiting until your customers leave? Why not interview them on a regular basis, when they are still your customers, so you can find out their unmet needs?"

From my years of asking company executives, I can report that only ten percent of companies take a structured approach when they try to learn about their competition. That means ninety percent do not. To me, that's equivalent to driving somewhere you've never been without directions, GPS, or a map. There's a pretty good chance you'll get lost. As we discussed in Chapter Two, most companies rely on their salespeople to be their sleuths, but the feedback they receive is not always reliable. Every company needs a disciplined plan to obtain competitive intelligence.

When I ask clients to create marketing messages that compare themselves to their top competitors, most cannot. Even if I give them the following example, "We have twenty-five percent more customer service reps than our competition," most can't. I ask them, "Can you make such a comparison? Do you know what your competitors have?" They cannot come up with the most basic comparative statements because they have little or no competitive intelligence.

I try to remind my clients of two simple rules. They are:

- Know what you *have* and what the competition *lacks.*
- Know what the competition *has* and you *lack.*

Having this intelligence is crucial. It's as important as knowing other vital business information such as how much inventory you have on hand, your raw material costs, and the amount of your fixed rental costs. Without solid, up-to-date competitive intelligence, you cannot make relevant operational decisions, you risk staying in second place (or third or fourth); you cannot convince your prospects that you are better than your competitors.

Get competitive intelligence from your customers, vendors, and subcontractors.

Include questions about your competitors in your customer research surveys.

Make phone calls to some of your good customers. They can give you a great deal of insightful information.

Vendors and subcontractors can be potential great sources of information about your competitors. They know the industry and have invaluable inside information on all the players. Meet with them and pick their brains. Many will be happy to speak with you.

A client told me that when he asked his customers about a competitor, he learned that they had shaved a week off the time it took them to deliver their products. With that information, my client focused on how to speed up his production, match his rival's delivery time, and negate their competitive advantage.

Also, consider using competitive intelligence to support strategic and tactical decisions that enhance your capacity for relevant selling. Few companies obtain this fundamental piece of the puzzle before they leap into the unknown. Not getting competitive intelligence is risky business, literally!

Please note competitive intelligence is different from the double blind research we have discussed throughout this book, although it may sometimes include it. Wikipedia describes competitive intelligence as an "ethical business practice as opposed to industrial espionage" and its focus is on the external business environment. It might help you determine the size and characteristics of a new market as well as the competition and what they do well or execute poorly, for example. It can provide "early signal" analysis.

Wikipedia goes on to say "marketing research is a tactical, methods-driven field that consists mainly of neutral primary research that draws on customer data in the form of beliefs and perceptions," whereas competitive intelligence "draws on a wider variety of sources from a wider range of stakeholders (e.g. suppliers, competitors, media, etc.)"

My experience has revealed that very few small- to medium-size businesses invest in either market research or competitive intelligence, to their own detriment. Both disciplines can help companies make better decisions.

WHO, HOW, AND WHERE

Most companies do not have a disciplined approach to gathering the unbiased voice of their customers. There are a number of ways to create such an approach, some better than others. But not doing anything is worse.

- Who, specifically, in your organization is responsible for obtaining the voice of the customer? The most common answer to this question is "everyone," but that's not how it really works in practice. That answer describes a corporate cultural mindset, not a functional assignment. Ideally, it *is* a functional assignment.
- So again, who, specifically, is responsible for finding out, analyzing, and disseminating your customers' and prospects' buying criteria? Who is your Chief Competitive Intelligence Officer? Not how good you are (that's customer satisfaction), but what they want from you. It's quite possible, and acceptable, that the answer is the same for both types of customer feedback.
- If you can't answer the previous question, who can? How does the answer relate to and impact your job?
- Who in your organization hires interns? Who has the best connections to the local post-secondary schools?
- What associations or peer groups does your company belong to? Can you tap those sources for market research?

- Has your organization done an online survey recently? If so, *what changed* as result of the survey data? If you answered, "little or nothing," that's common. What might you change in your next survey?
- If you have *not* done an online survey recently, who in your organization is best suited to take a stab at running the free online surveys we described? If you can't dive in, at least get your feet wet.

CHAPTER 10

How to Buy the Voice of Your Customer

You Get What You Pay For

WE'RE ALL FAMILIAR WITH THE CLICHÉ, "IF YOU needed brain surgery, you probably wouldn't think of shopping for the lowest priced surgeon." However, when companies think about having market research conducted, their decisions are often based on price. If your company wants to increase market share or margins, or the recession has done a number on your balance sheet, then you need expert services. Don't mess around with your business's health. Consider the gold standard in customer market research: hire a professional market research firm. While Smart Advantage provides the front end (extensive identification of potential competitive advantages and disadvantages, with double-blind survey design), and the back end (analysis, and operational and marketing implications), we always use a professional market research firm to conduct the field work: the actual telephone interviews, and the collection and tabulation of the responses.

Among other benefits, a professional firm will ensure that your survey is double-blind. Their call centers are experts at getting people to respond to telephone surveys. They can recognize well-crafted surveys, and/or offer help to fix one. They already have the programs in place to make sure the respondents fit your criteria, and the attributes are randomized when they should be to avoid order bias. They will run the cross-tabulations you need to compare your customers and prospects, or different sized customers, or decision makers and influencers; and they'll put the information into a form you can understand.

If you decide to hire a professional market research firm, how do you find one? How do you know what to ask for? How do you ensure you get what you want? What's your role in this effort?

Customer market research is not regulated by any government agencies. But the Council of American Survey Research Organizations (CASRO), which has over three hundred members, has a Code of Standards and Ethics with which its members must comply. The Market Research Association (MRA) is made up of companies that specialize in data gathering and they have a Blue Book directory that you can access online.

The American Marketing Association (AMA) has a Green Book directory with listing for all the major market research consulting firms in the United States. The Market Research Global Alliance (MRGA) enables its over 17,000 market-researcher members worldwide to connect, refer business to one another, and achieve their market research goals. It is the largest market research industry social network.

Let's talk about what you need to do to find the right resources and let's discuss the internal changes you may have to implement to ensure that your investment pays off. Since you and your staff members are probably occupied full time working *in* the business, and this is actually an *on*-the-business effort, it's best to have an internal champion. That champion will have to wear many hats: gatekeeper, facilitator, project manager, motivator, subject matter expert (by default), dispatcher, and even bottleneck at times. Since the champion's role is so critical, some forward-thinking organizations have a full-time a chief competitive intelligence officer handle this role. Others simply identify a person who can multitask and has great big-picture skills.

Next, clearly articulate your topic and your objective. Identify precisely what you want the research to discover and why. I know that this is easy to say, but hard to do. I suggest that your topic should be your target market's hierarchy of buying criteria – what they value most when they make their buying decisions. Your objective should be to come away with an unambiguous list of attributes that are ranked in order from most important to least important. Then make a firm internal commitment to act on the research results, regardless of what the results show!

METHODS

Decide on the surveying method that would be best for your research. The most common methods are interviewing by telephone, Computer Assisted Telephone Interviewing (CATI), Interactive Voice Response (IVR), online based, and snail mail. Here's a description of each:

Telephone. Interviewers phone respondents, ask them questions from a pre-written questionnaire and record the answers.

CATI. In this telephone surveying technique, the interviewer follows a script provided by a software application. This structured system speeds up the collection and editing of micro data because the software is able to customize the flow of the questionnaire based on the answers provided as well as information already known about the respondent. This is the method used for all the research studies I've described in *Relevant Selling*.

IVR. Respondents are contacted by mail, email, or

telephone and invited to call a telephone number to participate in a survey. Respondents give their survey responses to questions by using their phones' touch pads or their own voices.

Online. (Also known as Computer Assisted Web Interviewing, or CAWI. You can guess why *that* acronym hasn't stuck!) Respondents answer questions in an email or on a web site. Participants may be invited to respond to these online surveys by telephone calls, emails, or direct mail; or simply by open-ended broadcast, newspaper, or website appeals.

RETURNS

In the last chapter we discussed reliability: error rate and confidence level. For your survey, decide on the error rate and degree of confidence you will accept. Basically, this means the degree of accuracy you want and how dependable and reliable it must be. When you interview more respondents, you can get a lower rate of error and/or a higher confidence level. However, interviewing more people will cost more.

I'm generally satisfied with a ten percent error rate and a ninety percent confidence level. Both can be achieved when you receive at least 68 responses regardless of the size of the target population you are surveying. However, don't try to cut those 68 into smaller slices, because the error rate will go up and/or the confidence level will drop.

For example, if you interview a total of 68 respondents, half customers and half prospects, you will learn what 34 customers value and what 34 prospects value. When you get only 34 responses, the error rate will increase to about seventeen percent (at a ninety percent confidence level). If you want to maintain a ten percent error rate at a ninety percent confidence level for *prospects*, you need responses from 68 *prospects*.

It's tempting to try to survey a few customers from each of three or six or nine regions of the country. That's all right if you want to get a representative cross-section, but the comparison of the few responses from a given region to the responses from a different region will not give you a high a degree of statistical validity and may not be projectable.

Political pollsters typically prefer a three to four percent error rate and a ninety-five percent confidence level. To get those results, a survey must have more than 1,000 responses. No wonder political candidates must raise so much money!

Here's a hint. We generally recommend that our smaller B2B clients get 100 completed responses, composed of 50 of each "cohort." [Cohorts can be customers and prospects, or decision makers and influencers, or students and non-students, or men and women; any pair with a distinct difference, but still within your target market.] That results in an overall error rate of 8.2 percent, and lets us compare the two cohorts with an error rate of 11.6 percent, while still keeping the cost within reason.

You can plug in your own numbers at custominsight.
com/articles/random-sample-calculator.asp.

To find potential respondents, use your Customer
Relations Management (CRM) database. You can also
select respondents from your sales force's prospect and
customer lists or by purchasing lists. If you buy lists, be
careful, because they may often be out of date or inaccurate. Try to find out from the list vendor how and
when the database was prepared. Industry association membership rosters are also an excellent source of
potential contact names. Market research firms can also
obtain lists of potential interview candidates, sometimes
of better quality and at a lower cost than you can get (it's
a benefit of being in the business).

Before you purchase a list, make sure it contains
contact information for all respondents. Telephone
numbers are all you need for phone and CATI surveys;
email addresses are enough for online surveys. However,
the database vendor may have additional targeting
information that could prove useful to you (sometimes
for an additional fee). Such information might include
geographic region, gender, age, household income, and/
or purchasing/behavioral characteristics.

FINDING FIRMS

The best ways to find reliable research firms are through
referrals and prior use. You can also find them through

the yellow pages and Internet search engines. An online directory called the Green Book (at greenbook.org) lists many market research firms. Green Book's homepage is a bit dizzying. It lists over twenty different categories of firms. Chances are that you will be interested in "Data Collection – Interviewing," but when you click on it, you will have to sift through nearly 150 descriptions of firms, ads, and entries for related resources and services. (Of course, there is one more good source for reliable market research firms; you can contact us at Smart Advantage: info@smartadvantage.com.)

Firms conduct two distinctive types of research—qualitative and quantitative.

Qualitative research is not numbers oriented; it is more focused on obtaining addition insights from direct probing. This type of information is collected via discussion groups (focus groups) and/or in-depth one-on-one interviews. Focus groups are excellent for idea generation, helping to evaluate new communication campaigns, and to gain greater insight into how and why people do things. Often focus groups are used to evaluate new product designs or features. Focus groups are also used by pollsters to get a sense of the local electorate, partly because they can probe deeper into interesting or controversial topics, with what amount to group interviews.

Quantitative research, as its name implies, relies on numbers and having a reasonable number of completed interviews. This research is best when you are trying to project findings and when you may want or need to dig into the data a little deeper and look at various subgroups aside from just the overall total. What we have described in our case studies throughout this book has been quantitative research. The survey tool of choice would be a questionnaire consisting of structured answer choices along with a few open-ended questions.

SOCIAL NETWORKS

Many of my clients and audiences ask about using social networks for customer market research. For quantitative research like we just discussed, social networks don't work well. Again, not everyone has internet access; the members are self-selected, meaning they *decide on their own* to participate; not everyone agrees to participate in a survey even if they are a member; and it's almost impossible to ensure that the actual respondent belongs in your target market and is not just some grade school kid.

For qualitative research, however, social networks and on-line communities have become major sources of feedback because their members tend to accept what their fellow network members say and endorse. I discussed some of the risks and vulnerabilities of social networks in Chapter Two, and we discussed Starbucks' new "My Starbucks Idea" in Chapter Three. The Bank of America debit card fiasco we discussed in the last chapter went viral on social networks.

It is possible to quantify some social network feedback, but only by tracking comments and aggregating them into useful categories. For example, you could count positive and negative comments, event-based comments, product or service complaints, and requests and suggestions. Over time, you may be able to gain a sense of what your customers value, and how they perceive you. Having said that, carefully using these other forms of feedback is better than not seeking the voice of your customer at all.

Alan Appelbaum, president and CEO of Market Probe International, Inc., told me a great story that illustrates that when you want to conduct surveys, you get what you pay for. The moral is that if you cut corners, you'll compromise the quality of the data you collect.

Alan's firm bid on a large study to evaluate the design characteristics of a number of mobile communication products. The study called for the winning bidder to complete 500 interviews over a five-day period at a midtown Manhattan hotel. As often occurs, the client decided to go with the lowest bid, which had been submitted by a competitor – XYZ Market Research Firm (name changed to protect the guilty). Some preliminary work was done, but when XYZ was asked to sign a written contract, they refused.

So the client went back to Market Probe International and awarded them the job.

The day after Market Probe International received the

award, Alan called XYZ to try to get some background information. He was told that both of the executives who had set up the study had been fired, which left Market Probe International no background information whatsoever. Then, as Market Probe International got deeper into the study, they discovered the reason their client originally received such a lowball bid. XYZ had recruited candidates directly from Craigslist and offered a $75 incentive to those who completed the study. When XYZ got close to 600 responses – a hundred more than were needed – they told all the candidates they had recruited that the project was off. Then, after waiting a few days, XYZ reposted their solicitation for recruits for the very same study, but this time they offered only $50. Once again, over 500 interview candidates signed up. So XYZ assumed they had the necessary interview candidates without any further effort or expense.

But XYZ had absolutely no physical interaction with the proposed candidates; they had handled the entire process electronically. So XYZ didn't know that many were not qualified to participate. Alan said, "When we entered the picture and realized what had occurred, we informed the client that we could not accept the recruits without at least phone verification. The client agreed, and as a result of the verification process, Market Probe International had to replace over one hundred of the people initially recruited, who clearly were not qualified to respond to the survey we were about to conduct."

Believe it or not, it gets worse. Remember the "no

background information?" Market Probe International didn't know that XYZ had set up an electronic appointment confirmation system, and neglected to cancel it. "So we wound up having many more people show up who expected to participate in the survey," Alan laments. "And of course, some of them clearly were not qualified to begin with and even seemed to be homeless! It was chaotic and quite stressful, but we were able to overcome all of these challenges. Basically, to avoid any confrontations we paid the unqualified candidates, but later we pulled the data for those individuals out of the final data set because we could not, in good conscience, deliver their data to our client."

It is true that you get what you pay for. I realize not all companies have a budget for this kind of research. I recommend to my clients that voice of the customer research should be in the budget every year. But if you cannot afford research as we described it here, getting feedback as described in Chapter Nine is better than doing nothing to learn what your customers value. It can make or break your growth efforts.

CHECKLIST FOR PROSPECTIVE RESEARCH FIRMS

Before you hire a professional research firm, interview different candidates. Meet with them personally and question them. Don't be bashful, and remember that you will be entrusting the firm you hire to uncover information that is vital to your business. Before you meet with and interview firms, prepare a list of questions. Discuss those questions with your staff and get their insights and opinions. They may point out concerns that you overlooked.

Here are a few questions to get you started. Use them as a guide and add specific questions that may be important to you. When you question research firms, make sure that you fully understand their answers. If you don't, ask them to clarify their answers for you.

- If I provide contact lists, what form is acceptable? (Most firms want an Excel spreadsheet.)
- How long do you anticipate the fieldwork will take?
- How often will you update me on fieldwork progress?
- What happens if you are unable to get the contracted number of completed interviews?
- Do you provide a summary report?
- Will your summary report include implications for my organization (operations, marketing, sales, etc.) or just a summary of the results?

AND THAT'S A WRAP...

My hope is you have enjoyed this book as you "met" some of our clients and joined them on their journeys to relevant selling. I also expect that you will look at and listen to marketing and sales messages with a bit more of a critical view. Regardless of your "corporate" position, you are always a customer. I always ask someone I am buying a product or a service from, "why should I buy from you?" I challenge others to become skilled at relevant selling. And more importantly, I encourage them to listen to us, *their* customers.

As customers we can find irrelevant selling everywhere. I go to a hairdresser who serves a large number of professional men and women. Many places can deliver a good haircut. But if I have to wait five, ten minutes for the stylist, why do I always have to read *Vogue* and gossip magazines? Wouldn't it be nice to see a *Business Week* or *Forbes* offered? A small way to be more relevant lets the customer know you care about what they care about.

I live in Florida where the sun shines year round. But a few years ago I went shopping for a new patio set in November. Guess what? Not available. Most of the stores who sell outdoor furniture, including Home Depot, think it is just a summer item. Well, if you live in Vermont that's certainly true. These stores make nationwide selling decisions apparently not relevant to geographic needs.

USA Today did a series of interviews with four luxury car brand top execs: Cadillac, Lexus, BMW, and Hyundai. The main question was how "luxury" is defined in the car world. What struck me about this article is that all four executives had very different answers, ranging from brand reputation to service; performance to craftsmanship and so on. Not one said "our customers tell us it is…." If we are trying to define luxury cars, wouldn't the buyers of luxury cars have a better idea?

Too many businesses want to believe the customer wants what they have to sell, e.g. high performance over service levels and reliability. Even though Consumer Reports surveys customers all the time, I can't help but wonder why auto manufacturers aren't all getting five stars in the areas of customer importance.

Too many businesses try a one-size fits all approach

for their customers and many do just fine in spite of it. I am not suggesting you expand your product offerings but I am saying sell with a high degree of relevance and be more profitable. Stay very closely and frequently tuned to what your customers value and you will have an easier time holding on to precious margins and market share.

SMART ADVANTAGE...

If you enjoyed the journeys our clients have taken with us and would like to begin your own experience to becoming more and more relevant, we would love to help you. You might even be in the next book!

We have a free newsletter, opt-in only. If you would like to subscribe, you can sign up on the home page of our website, www.smartadvantage.com.

Smart Advantage consultants deliver a very specialized process that enables companies to identify potential differentiators they don't even know they have. We help them find which ones are *relevant*. We then turn it into powerful marketing and sales messaging complete with identification of operational considerations that will support the customer relevance.

The majority of our clients close about twenty to forty percent more in sales within the first few months of full implementation. We are the only consultancy specializing in this proprietary process. We frequently stay with a client, often at our own expense, until the results show up.

Hundreds of companies have changed their messaging as a result of our work. I have taught over 4,000 CEO's in over 400 industries how to uncover and articulate their differentiators. Smart Advantage has designed and analyzed over 200 market research surveys, all with the primary objective of finding relevance.

If you're now convinced that you need to identify you relevant competitive advantages based on double-blind market research, and you would like some help, you might be pleased to know this is what we do at Smart Advantage. Contact us at info@smartadvantage.com, or 954-763-5757.

INDEX